Praise for

The HR Renaissance

"In this smart and practical book, Jathan Janove redefines the role of HR in modern organizations. By shifting focus from compliance to culture, he offers a refreshing and effective approach to people management."

—DANIEL H. PINK, #1 *New York Times* best-selling author of *The Power of Regret, Drive,* and *To Sell Is Human*

"This book is a crucial guide for any HR professional looking to evolve from the traditional role of compliance enforcer to a transformative leader in culture and human capital strategy. Expertly blending extensive experience with practical insights, Jathan shows exactly how to shift focus from risk aversion to building thriving workplace cultures that prioritize human potential. This book isn't just theoretical—it's a road map filled with actionable steps, real-world examples, and strategies to navigate the complex landscape of modern HR. Whether you're a seasoned HR leader or just starting in the field, this book will equip you with the tools needed to make a lasting impact on your organization's culture and success."

—DR. MARSHALL GOLDSMITH, Thinkers50 #1 Executive Coach; *New York Times* best-selling author of *The Earned Life, Triggers,* and *What Got You Here Won't Get You There*

"The superpower of connected and collaborative human resources is the key to creating our 'Working Together' leadership and management system to create value for all the stakeholders and the greater good! Thank you, Jathan, for your thoughts about how to improve the support of our human resources!"

—**ALAN MULALLY,** former CEO, Boeing Commercial Airplanes; former CEO, the Ford Motor Company

"We engaged Jathan to write the 'Putting Humanity into HR Compliance' column as part of SHRM's initiative to promote workplace civility. This book provides a readable road map for how to make HR organizationally indispensable. CEOs should read it too!"

—**JOHNNY C. TAYLOR,** Jr., SHRM-SCP, President and CEO, Society for Human Resource Management (SHRM)

"A fast-changing world demands enlightened human resource thinking and practices. Leveraging his vast training and experience, Jathan Janove brings that thinking to life in a very approachable fashion. A very worthy read for any aspiring leader."

—**DOUGLAS R. CONANT,** retired CEO, Campbell Soup Company; best-selling author; founder, Conant Leadership

"A strong company culture plays a crucial role in driving business performance and achieving long-term success. Jathan understands this better than anybody, and I'm so glad he shares his wisdom with us in this book. His insights are invaluable, and this book is a must-read for all Human Resources leaders!"

—**TRACY STACHNIAK,** Chief Human Resources Officer, Toyota Material Handling, Inc.

"Culture is the number one reason a person stays at or leaves a company. However, HR continues to focus on factors and tactics that are outside the scope of culture. This must change. Jathan has not only captured this reality, but he's shown a tangible path for HR to step into leading from a people-first and culture-based lens. It's the wake-up call HR needs because we have a fantastic opportunity to step in to move our company's forward through our people!"

—**STEVE BROWNE,** SHRM-SCP, Chief People Officer, LaRosa's, Inc.; author of *HR on Purpose!!, HR Rising!!,* and *HR Unleashed!!*

"I have nothing but the highest praise for Jathan's indispensable book! Every leader uses HR skills, every day, in every interaction. This practical book can be used by every leader to transform themselves and their team's culture in extraordinary ways. It's truly life changing!"

—**CHERIE FOSTER,** MD, Specialty Medical Officer, Pediatrix Medical Group, Division Chief of Neonatology, Joe DiMaggio Children's Hospital

"Wonderful stories! I love how Jathan thinks about HR and the possibility to be an advisor and coach not just trusted, but driving business results at the highest levels of every organization. He understands it is our duty to help businesses understand the strategic importance of the humans they employ. I'm excited about the conversations this book will drive within our profession."

—**LOUONNA KACHUR,** Global Human Resources Director, EnerSys

"Jathan Janove's newest book captures his passion about strategic HR leadership and the changing role of the human resources discipline in moving companies forward. His unique perspective—first, as a long-term employment attorney and then as an executive coach and management consultant—helps him provide objective insight and practical tools into a reinvented HR role that includes legal compliance but, more importantly, drives leadership with a heart. If you're looking to scale your company and drive greater employee engagement and discretionary effort, follow his wisdom to move your HR practice from compliance cop to culture coach—and your organizational culture from formal and distant to collaborative and empathetic."

—**PAUL FALCONE,** former CHRO of Nickelodeon Animation Studios; author of the Paul Falcone Workplace Leadership series

"As an HR Leader, I've always disliked being the 'no police.' Jathan's book offers a refreshing perspective, guiding HR professionals with real-life examples and practical tools to shift the focus from saying 'no' to finding ways to say 'yes.' It's not just about policy enforcement but about building a coaching culture within the HR team. Jathan has articulated in clear and actionable terms what I've been striving to achieve in HR for years. I'm excited to share this book with my team!"

—**CRYSTAL KOHANKE,** MS, SHRM-CP, Certified Coach; SVP and Chief People Officer, Arkansas Children's

"This book's wisdom and practical tools are equally applicable from high growth startup organizations to mature Fortune 1000 companies. I only wish that I and the HR managers with whom I've worked over the last few decades had identified and integrated comparable practices."

—**EDITH DORSEN,** Managing Director, Women's Venture Capital Fund

"Today's workplace requires policy, practices, and broad positive actions that create a supportive culture producing outstanding individual and organizational results. Jathan captures this need in his forward thinking 'coaching not compliance.' The book's leadership principles of teamwork, collaboration, and cooperation breed success!"

—**KAY TORAN,** President and CEO, Volunteers of America—Oregon

"Jathan masterfully redefines HR from compliance-driven enforcer to dynamic culture coach. He demonstrates that an employee-centered approach—focused on civility, respect, and dignity—surpasses traditional risk prevention models and offers a mutually beneficial environment for growth and success. From the compelling Star Profile to his innovative, people-centered developmental strategies, Jathan nails it! A must-read for those committed to transforming HR into a force for positive, meaningful good."

—**PETE WONG,** Chief HR Officer,
AZ Athletic Associates LLC; former VP-HR,
Phoenix Suns and Arizona Diamondbacks

"In this highly engaging and useful book, Jathan re-thinks traditional HR practices and reveals how the punitive, manipulative, bureaucratic style that has come to characterize so much of modern HR serves no one. Using lots of practical examples, Jathan sets out a humane, honest, caring, and direct approach that serves both employer and employee. This is a must read for every HR professional who is open to rethinking the basics."

—**PAUL BUCHANAN,** employment law attorney and
partner, Buchanan Angeli Altschul & Sullivan LLP

"Jathan is thinking ahead of the intersection between legal affairs and day-to-day HR operations. This is what makes Jathan a thought leader in the HR profession. This book provides practical, usable advice without being condescending or authoritarian. Having those coaching conversations before there is a problem, walking the walk and talking the talk is what Jathan counsels. Read this book!"

—**BRENDA RUSHFORTH,** SHRM-SCP, Vice President
& Chief Human Resources Officer, Chapman University

"Jathan Janove is to every HR director what Bill James is to every Major League Baseball General Manager. Jathan is telling us how to think differently about how to manage our biggest asset—our employees. He has given us a playbook to change the rules of engagement for the employee/employer relationship. Every HR Director and every CEO should read this book. It will guide you to a better employee/employer experience, a better culture, and drive better employee retention."

—**RICH STAYNER,** retired CEO,
Bridge Property Management

"Jathan has done a masterful job of capturing the realities of common ways we 'kill' good culture in companies. He provides wonderful coaching practices and simple but very effective tools that really create an environment and culture of trust, respect, appreciation, and confidence. Every HR professional needs to read this book and apply its teachings. It truly will transform Human Resource Management, eliminating the long held negative stigmas causing people to avoid HR. Instead, they'll be replaced with gratitude and respect causing people and leaders to actively seek out HR!"

—**PAUL A. JONES,** Chief People Officer,
USANA Health Sciences, Inc.

"Having a positive culture really means focusing on behaviors that are acceptable and extinguishing the other behaviors. Culture is the lure to catch the real concerns, real frustrations, and real opportunities to celebrate. This book is full of deep experiences and wisdom that if taken to heart will help design a company culture that impacts individuals in powerful ways."

—**BRIAN ROSENBERG,** PhD, Executive Director, Office of Professional Fulfillment and Wellbeing, Pediatrix Medical Group

"As the head of one of the world's largest coaching organizations, I am excited about Jathan's book. Shifting HR's focus from compliance to coaching will prove greatly beneficial to organization health and employee growth."

—**BRANDON MERGARD,** CEO, Marshall Goldsmith Stakeholder Centered Coaching

"Jathan's wisdom and passion for what he does is evident in this book. I believe it will be a valuable tool for anyone looking to improve the employee experience in the workplace and is something that our organization will continue to benefit from as he coaches the next generation of our leaders."

—**PATRICIA DANIELS,** Executive Director, Constructing Hope

"This book inspires us to consider how effective HR practices are the backbone in any organization looking to unlock the full potential of their workforce. HR can and should serve as a catalyst for transforming human capital into a strategic organizational advantage."

—**SYDNEY WILLIAMS**, PhD, President, Designetics, Inc.

"When I was a corporate CEO, I was fortunate to have Jathan as my employment law counsel. His impact went well beyond just keeping us out of legal trouble. I'm glad he has captured what he did for us in a book. Read it!"

—**JIM GREENBAUM**, former CEO, Access Long Distance Co.; Managing Director, Greenbaum Foundation

"HR is on the threshold of transformation from a compliance-oriented cost center to that of human capital strategists who can unleash the potential of employees' hearts and minds. This book provides us with the tools necessary to complete this transformation."

—**BRUCE CUTRIGHT**, retired CHRO, Mary Lanning Healthcare

"This book is full of practical wisdom and tools that enable HR professionals to bring the 'human' back into the important work of HR, especially in a time when many people feel our culture is so polarized. This book provides a sound voice of reason to help us provide more inclusive, humane, and civil workplaces and cultures. I highly recommend it."

—**COLLEEN J. MCMANUS**, HR executive, coach, and consultant; Phoenix, AZ

"This book inspires HR professionals to pursue their work with humanity as well as strategic acumen. A great combination for success in the workplace!"

—DR. ISAAC DIXON, Interim Chief People Officer, Oregon Health & Science University (OHSU)

"Jathan's book offers a compelling vision for HR professionals seeking to break free from the constraints of compliance and become catalysts for positive organizational change. With his expert guidance, readers will discover how to shift from rule enforcement to nurturing a thriving company culture that inspires employees and drives success."

—JEFF LIDDY, President, The Father's Table

"In *The HR Renaissance*, Jathan Janove redefines HR for a new era, shifting from compliance to fostering thriving cultures. His actionable insights empower CHROs to become key drivers of organizational success, blending human potential with strategic growth. A must-read for leaders dedicated to creating high-performance, people-centered workplaces."

—CRYSTAL MAGGELET, CEO and Chairperson of the Board, FJ Management Inc.

"As a former employment defense lawyer turned California plaintiffs' advocate, I've seen how fear-based HR practices backfire. Jathan lays out a compelling, practical path toward culture-first leadership—and it's long overdue."

—JEFF RANEN, founding partner,
Atticus Law Group, Los Angeles

"Implementing Jathan's teachings and coaching over the past thirty years positively transformed our management–employee culture. Results have led to continual progressive cohesiveness and performance, providing vastly improved bottom-line results. Follow this book's advice, and your company will benefit immensely."

—IRA FIELD, retired CEO/
Chairman, Steel Encounters

THE

HR

RENAISSANCE

JATHAN JANOVE

THE

HR

RENAISSANCE

TRANSFORMING
FROM LEGAL GUARD
TO GROWTH PARTNER

FC

**FAST
COMPANY**
Press

An Inc. Original
New York, New York
www.anincoriginal.com

Copyright © 2025 Jathan Janove

This work is being published under the An Inc. Original imprint by an exclusive arrangement with Inc. Magazine. Inc. Magazine and the Inc. logo are registered trademarks of Mansueto Ventures, LLC. The An Inc. Original logo is a wholly owned trademark of Mansueto Ventures, LLC.

Distributed by River Grove Books

Design and composition by Greenleaf Book Group and Teresa Muñiz
Cover design by Greenleaf Book Group and Teresa Muñiz

Publisher's Cataloging-in-Publication data is available.

Paperback ISBN: 978-1-63909-060-0

Hardcover ISBN: 978-1-63909-061-7

eBook ISBN: 978-1-63909-062-4

First Edition

This book is dedicated to the late Steve Beeley, a crusty mentor who despite continually expressing his dislike of attorneys, played a pivotal role in the workplace-focused career I've enjoyed.

Contents

INTRODUCTION: HR'S WRONG TURN AND
HOW TO MAKE IT RIGHT   1

CHAPTER 1: A New Vision: HR as an Investment vs.
Cost Center   13

CHAPTER 2: Reshaping the HR Profession   29

CHAPTER 3: The Best Defense Is a Good Coach 49

CHAPTER 4: Think "Communication" Instead
of "Documentation".   69

CHAPTER 5: A Performance Management System That
Works Better for Employers Than Lawyers   83

CHAPTER 6: It's Time to Fire "Progressive" Discipline 99

CHAPTER 7: Improve Hiring and Promotion by Avoiding
the "Stupid Switch"   113

CHAPTER 8: No More Tomes!: Simplifying Policies
and Onboarding.   127

CHAPTER 9: Minimize Harassment by Focusing on Civility,
Not the Law   139

CHAPTER 10: Inclusion: Replace Preaching with Practice. . . .   151

CONCLUSION   161

THE HR RENAISSANCE

ACKNOWLEDGMENTS   165

NOTES   167

ABOUT THE AUTHOR   173

OTHER BOOKS BY THE AUTHOR   175

HR's Wrong Turn and How to Make It Right

"Do you love your job?"

That's the question I ask other HR professionals when we meet. Their answer tells me instantly how their organization views the role of Human Resources.

If they tell me no—and that's most people these days—then I know their organization uses HR primarily as an enforcer of intricate organization policies and rules. HR is essentially a Compliance Cop. In these organizations, leaders treat HR as little more than a cost of doing business—like taxes you must pay. As a result, these leaders take a passive approach to the HR function: "Let them do their compliance thing without hopefully costing us too much money."

The small percentage of people who say, "Yes, I love my job" reveal to me that their organization has embraced a different role for HR, that of Culture Coach. These organizations recognize that human beings make the primary difference in an organization's success or failure and that workplace culture is hugely important. To them, "Human Resources" isn't a *cost*; it is an *investment* in maximizing human capital.

Compliance Cops are primarily responsible for preventing or defending legal claims. Culture Coaches are responsible for improving business success.

How about you? How would you answer that question? If you're the head of HR in your company, how do you think your staff would answer the question?

Reflecting on my forty-five-year career in this field, first as an attorney and then as an executive leadership coach and organization development consultant, it strikes me that somewhere, the profession made a wrong turn, which, to this day, has produced unfortunate consequences. I hope this book will help steer the direction toward the positive contributions made by Culture Coaches.

A WITNESS TO HR'S WRONG TURN

Employment law claims began to be a thing following the passage of the Civil Rights Act in 1964. Claims grew slowly in the 1970s and picked up steam in the 1980s, especially after the US Supreme Court ruled that sexual harassment is legally actionable. Workplace claims exploded in the 1990s, including new federal, state, statutory, regulatory, and common law claims. Matching this explosion were career opportunities for HR professionals and lawyers like me.

In a way, I got lucky because I witnessed this explosion firsthand. As a first-year law student at the University of Chicago in 1980, I received a summer grant to study the newly created Illinois Human Rights Commission. I also worked in the new Employment Discrimination section of the Mandel Legal Aid Clinic, which continued throughout law school. I handled claims of sex and race discrimination and harassment, wrongful discharge, and unlawful retaliation.

In the early 1980s, you had traditional labor lawyers and personnel departments while the HR and employment lawyer professions were nascent. Employment law was just beginning to wax as traditional labor law continued to wane.

Following graduation in 1982, I joined a corporate law firm in Salt Lake City. An employment law claim came to the firm for representation. None of the lawyers had ever handled such a claim, so it got passed to me, the newbie associate attorney. Before even making partner, I was the firm's leader of a burgeoning employment law practice.

Then, I founded a management-side employment law firm in the early 1990s. At conferences, I learned that one of the most effective ways to pick up new clients was to scare the heck out of them. I became adept at telling nightmarish war stories—the worst of the worst. This approach, which to this day is still employed by lots of other management-side attorneys, contributed heavily to HR becoming a risk-averse, compliance-obsessed function. The central goal became: Don't get sued. This led to endless, mind-numbing, and disengaging trainings; hundred-page handbooks; innumerable forms, procedures, processes, and documentation; and so on.

The game became compliance, claim prevention, and claim defense. Knowledge of employment law was paramount. Lost was humanity. Every employee became a potential plaintiff, someone to protect the company against.

To protect employers from employees who might take advantage of leave policies, including leaves mandated under state and federal law, the plan was to document the heck out of every request and make employees jump through every hoop the employer could legally impose.

Clever plaintiffs' lawyers started coming up with implied contract claims, so we defense lawyers recommended blasting employees with at-will and contractual disclaimers. We'd put them in our handbooks, include them in new employee orientation signoffs, and remind employees of their lack of legal rights every chance we got.

The directive: "You must follow the rules in the handbook, but we have no obligation to do so." Also, "Please keep in mind that you can be fired without notice at any time for any reason or no reason." These disclaimers became ubiquitous. I almost expected to see one embossed on company toilet paper.

Another noxious practice that emerged was that any time we had a problem with a particular employee that hadn't yet been written about, we'd slap a policy on it. So what if it's only one employee out of a thousand. All thousand are now subject to the new policy. I once encountered a nineteen-page expense reimbursement policy and forms. Puh-lease!

To show that we were compliant and enable us to let our weakest employees go, we would implement a formal written annual performance program. The goal was not to develop, enable, assist, empower, or engage. It was to cover our you-know-whats.

To avoid the risk that a discharged employee would claim we made the termination decision for unlawful reasons, we implemented a rigid set of formal disciplinary procedures. Also, to avoid the risk of mischief during the exit, we'd march the discharged employee out the door like a dangerous convict being transferred from one prison to another.

THE COST OF CREATING COMPLIANCE COPS

As this obsession with compliance continued to build, cultural considerations got shoved to the side. Focusing on culture and human capital strategy, which, in my experience, comprise a far healthier approach for organizational success, got lost in the shuffle.

Speaking as a former plaintiffs' and then defense employment law attorney, I can say that there's a painful irony here. This claim avoidance approach has worked better for lawyers than employers. As a management attorney, my best clients billable-hour-wise were the ones most compliance-obsessed. Conversely, my worst clients billable-hour-wise had the healthiest cultures. But why?

Nearly two centuries ago, Edgar Allan Poe provided the answer. In "The Cask of Amontillado," he began the story with: "The thousand injuries of Fortunato, I had borne as I best could, but when he ventured upon insult, I vowed revenge."[1] Unfortunately, employers and the HR profession have largely overlooked this timeless piece of wisdom.

Early in my career, I learned the primary reason why disgruntled employees sought representation. It wasn't the "injury" such as the lost job, promotion denied, job transfer, etc. That's what we lawyers focused on. Rather, the motivation to sue came from something more basic: anger at how they were treated. Compliance-obsessed employers failed to realize that their approach created breeding grounds for this kind of anger—the feeling of being disrespected, dehumanized, degraded, and demoralized, so that when the injury came in whatever form, it generated a desire for revenge.

Here's another reason compliance obsession has backfired on employers: The more abundant your policies, procedures, forms, processes, etc., the harder it is to administer them correctly. I can't tell you the number of times my client's formal disciplinary procedures were used against it. Why? Because the managers failed to use them as designated. Instead, we had inconsistency—inconsistency in the treatment of similarly situated employees, inconsistency with policy and reality, and sometimes even inconsistency in the policies themselves. As a plaintiffs' attorney, I likened employer inconsistency to mother's milk. It went a long way to nurturing our claim.

Along these lines, one of my favorite studies comes from California, otherwise known as the Golden State for Lawyers. In an article published by the Society for Human Resource Management (SHRM), a San Francisco attorney did a simple word search for "performance evaluation" and "performance review" in published California state and federal court decisions over a six-month period.

She found forty cases where the performance review was cited by the court as a material fact. In thirty-nine of these cases, the review was cited not by the employer to support its defense. It was cited by the employee to prove their discrimination, harassment, or retaliation claim. In only one lonely case did the employer use it to bolster its defense.[2] How's that for claim prevention!

CULTURE COACHES TO THE RESCUE

The primary objective of this book is to persuade organization leaders to change the prevailing HR compliance paradigm into one of culture stewardship and human capital maximization. By investing time and energy in your HR function to convert it from Compliance Cop to Culture Coach, you will be able to create and preserve a healthy culture that maximizes human talent and energy aligned with what your organization needs to prosper.

Since Culture Coaches are few and far between, let me give you an example. In 2005, as chief human resources officer (CHRO) of Mary Lanning Healthcare, Bruce Cutright received a wake-up call that fundamentally changed his career. It happened during a board meeting. The hospital had been continually losing money. A very unhappy board chair told the CEO that things needed to change, or the CEO and the other senior team members would be replaced.

Up to that point, Bruce thought he was performing well. A self-developed guru of employment and benefits law, he focused on compliance, as was expected by the CEO. But the message was loud and clear. Something had to change. Bruce had to start thinking about improving the bottom line, or he needed to find another job. Bruce prided himself on defending the hospital against employment claims and considered it a badge of courage to show that he could handle tough employment situations. Conducting investigations and terminating problem employees were particular strengths. Yet, his hospital had a high turnover rate of 22 percent. First-year turnover was 48 percent. Almost 50 percent of new employees left the organization before one year of employment. The cost of employee turnover was enormous. Something had to change. Clearly, compliance alone was not working.

Bruce began in earnest to find a new way of doing things. He visited with multiple HR colleagues who shared similar stories. He looked for reward programs and a new pay-for-performance plan that would entice employees to stay longer and perform better. Bruce envisioned handing out rewards to star performers and buttons to signify the best performers. However, it wasn't until he met with a consultant from Gallup that he realized his approach was wrong.

She asked him questions about his approach to engaging employees. Did he solicit the opinions of employees? How did he select employees? What was the area of highest turnover? Bruce answered the last question by noting extremely high turnover in housekeeping. When the consultant asked why, he answered, "Because people don't grow up to be housekeepers."

She replied, "Some people do grow up to be housekeepers. It's your job to find them."

Bruce realized she was right, and from that time forward, he had to change his focus from compliance guru to human capital strategist. This transition was not easy. His CEO and other senior managers also had to recognize the need to redefine his role and expectations of the human resources function. Thus began the start of a long journey that transformed the organization from very low employee engagement, poor financial performance, high turnover, and mediocre customer satisfaction to repeatedly winning the Gallup Great Workplace Award.[3] This award is given annually to forty organizations worldwide that have demonstrated success in employee engagement. During Bruce's tenure at Mary Lanning Healthcare, it won the award eight times in a nine-year period.

Bruce recently shared with me this observation: "I lived on the dark side of employee relations before my transition to that of a human capital strategist. The actions I initiated to transform one organization have prompted me to become a strong advocate for redesigning the traditional compliance-focused HR function."[4]

FROM CRITICISM TO HOPE

This project began as a book of criticism about the Human Resources function in organizations today. I now consider it a book of hope.

Throughout the book, I share stories about actual people who have successfully transitioned from Cop to Coach. They are showing all of us how to make sure that HR plays an indispensable role in organizational success by helping to build a culture of constant improvement and high employee engagement. The stories I share exemplify both HR and overall organization leaders. You'll learn about people like Louonna Kachur and Max Neves, who, like

Bruce Cutright, are leading examples of HR Culture Coaches, and about organization leaders such as former Ford Motor Company CEO Alan Mulally and former Campbell Soup CEO Doug Conant, both of whom embraced a culture-first approach.

Their stories should persuade you that the transition can be made. The rest of the book shows how to do it—I describe specific concepts, strategies, and tools to enable the organization and its HR professionals to convert from Compliance Cop to Culture Coach. This book doesn't simply provide a theory; it includes the means to implement it.

The book starts with two chapters that present a new vision for the role of HR in an organization (Chapter 1) and the responsibilities that should be part of a Culture Coach working in the HR department (Chapter 2). Chapters 3 to 10 dive deeper into traditional HR functions and how they should be reshaped to be more consistent with a Culture Coach mentality that strives to make HR a value-added partner in the organization. I discuss the following HR functions:

- Maintaining a focus on compliance but with a Culture Coach twist (Chapter 3)

- Rethinking communication styles and tools (Chapter 4)

- Turning performance reviews into a process that helps people actually improve (Chapter 5)

- Replacing progressive discipline (where consequences escalate) with a truly "progressive" approach that focuses on solving problems and improving behavior (Chapter 6)

- Using a tool that simplifies and enhances hiring and promotion decisions (Chapter 7)
- Working to drastically simplify policies and how that impacts onboarding (Chapter 8)
- Focusing on civility to minimize harassment (Chapter 9)
- Implementing a truly inclusive environment (Chapter 10)

There is also a Conclusion to encourage you to become a true Culture Coach yourself. I don't think you'll be sorry if you do: I've met a great many HR Compliance Cops who aren't happy at work. By contrast, I've never met an HR Culture Coach who didn't love their job. This project began as a book of criticism. I now consider it a book of hope.

CHAPTER 1

A New Vision: HR as an Investment vs. Cost Center

You've probably heard the saying that "culture eats strategy for breakfast." It's an acknowledgment that the biggest determinant of what an organization achieves is how people interact and treat each other day in and day out rather than any formal statement of strategy or goals. I agree with the statement because I've seen it in action innumerable times.

The trick then becomes to have a culture that *supports* the business strategy and vision. Here's my definition of a culture that can fulfill that function:

A workplace suffused in trust, respect, civility, collaboration, transparency, performance expectations, accountability, and overall alignment with what the organization needs to succeed.

In this chapter, I talk about how HR can play a role in creating that kind of culture and the challenges organizations will face in getting leadership to appreciate that role.

USING HR TO DRIVE IMPROVEMENT

Perhaps no leader embodies the vision for how HR can move beyond enforcing compliance more than Alan Mullaly, who led Boeing from 1998 to 2006 and then Ford Motor Company from 2006 to 2014. His leadership strategy relied heavily on making Human Resources a partner at the C-suite to drive success rather than an enforcement arm of his organizations.

Under his tenure at these companies, Boeing's commercial aviation arm rebounded after being devastated by the attacks of September 11, 2001. Subsequently, Henry Ford's great-grandson hired Mulally to rescue Ford Motor Company from financial disaster. Mulally brought Ford from the brink of ruin to a leading position in the automotive industry. Ford's stock went from a low of $1 per share to more than $18 per share during his service, a 1,700 percent improvement. At a unionized company, his employee approval rating was over 90 percent. You can learn more of his story in the book *American Icon: Alan Mulally and the Fight to Save Ford Motor Company* by Bryce Hoffman.

Over the past three years, I've been fortunate to interview Mulally for SHRM publications and to exchange views with him via email. Mulally designed and nurtured what he calls a "Working Together" leadership and management system. He describes it as a system that creates value for all stakeholders and the greater good. People work together toward a compelling vision with a comprehensive strategy and a relentless implementation plan.

This includes making a commitment to a connected culture of love by design that supports, as Mulally recently shared with me, "a smart, healthy, psychologically safe, and high-performance organization based in humility, love, service and deep respect for all participants and stakeholders, where we help each other individually and as a team while continuing to grow and improve." He added, "And no group is more important and can make more of a difference in this continuous improvement than HR."[1]

Mulally told me that most corporate leaders undervalue the HR profession. "All too often, HR is not part of the leadership team. Yet it can and should be part of the leadership team *and* the process owner for everything associated with the employees, including recruitment, performance management and continuous leadership development. When the leadership team decides on organization goals, objectives, and initiatives, including what will be measured and when, HR's job is to hold all the elements of the company accountable for ensuring that they deeply understand and keep their commitments."[2]

At Ford, Mulally established weekly three-hour business process plan review (BPR) meetings. At these meetings, the person in charge of each department, group, or unit presented their team's goals and candidly shared the team's progress against the plan to support the organization's objectives. The other leaders then offered support, input, suggestions, and help.

"HR was a full, active member of our leadership team and our BPRs, which were critical to our success," Mulally shared with me. "Our HR leader knew everything about the business, whether it had to do with product development, finance, information technology, manufacturing or anything else of importance."[3]

Mulally is a huge proponent of personal development coaching, having been coached himself by Marshall Goldsmith. He told me, "If you work in HR for a company that supports coaching, you have a great job and opportunity to continuously improve the performance of the individuals and the team. In addition to your own coaching work, you get to vet and deploy coaches throughout the organization to serve."[4]

Mulally cites an example of a brilliant senior executive whose behaviors did not support his desired working-together culture. "Her response was," he says, "'This is how I was taught and what I've been around, and I've been very successful.'"

However, she was open to coaching. "We got her an executive coach," Mulally explained to me, "and did a 360-degree assessment. She focused on three behaviors to change and, as a result, became one of the most trusted, valued, and appreciated executives we had."[5]

In an email exchange with me in October 2024, SHRM President and CEO Johnny C. Taylor Jr., SHRM-SCP, had this to say: "When one hears directly from America's most successful CEOs that HR people matter to business, it makes clear that

SHRM's work to equip and prepare HR leaders with business and human capital knowledge is mission-critical now more than ever."[6]

FIXING THE CEO-HR DISCONNECT

Making HR a partner in achieving success won't happen until the vision of what HR is today and what it can be changes dramatically. The biggest hurdle may be the way most top leaders view HR, a.k.a. mostly as Compliance Cops rather than Culture Coaches. Consequently, there is a disconnect between what HR may want to accomplish—empowered, engaged, fully contributing employees—and what the C-suite demands ("avoid claims"). In this section, I share stories that illustrate this disconnect between CEOs and HR and discuss why resolving this disconnect has to be a starting point for any effort to transition HR into a Culture Coach mode.

The friction between HR and the C-suite is well-known to every senior HR professional I've ever talked to. Here are four quick examples.

Story #1: "I Hate HR!"

Several years ago, for an article, I interviewed senior executives, asking them what they thought about HR. My first interviewee ran a research and development operation (R&D) for a Fortune 50 company.

He began the interview with, "I hate HR!"

"Why?" I asked.

"I'm an engineer by trade," he said. "I get engineering. I get manufacturing. I'm a numbers guy and get accounting. I'm also a techno-geek and get IT. The one thing I *don't* get are human beings. So where I need the most help, I get the least. That's why I hate HR."

Story #2: An Ignored Seat at the Table

Another executive I interviewed was a member of the C-suite of a bank. He told me that the head of HR had the proverbial seat at the table. However, he wasn't sure she appreciated it.

"Why?" I asked.

"At every executive committee meeting," he said, "when the head of HR makes her presentation, I can't help but look over at the CEO and CFO. Almost every time, their jaws get slack and their eyelids droop . . . It's like it's their nap time."

Story #3: Can't Get No Respect

After speaking at an HR conference, I met an HR director who shared an experience with me.

> After it became clear to me and my HR team that our managers lacked basic communication skills, and that it was costing us in terms of employee engagement, retention, and contributing to employee claims and litigation, I put together a plan for communications and leadership skills training for our managers and supervisors.

However, because our HR staff was already stretched thin—I reported to a CFO who viewed HR as a cost to be contained—I needed outside resources to make the program work. I made my proposal to the CFO and CEO and requested a budget that I felt would ensure measurable progress.

I got back an approval for the project. But instead of the budget I requested, I was given $5,000—for the entire year!

The HR director then described how insult got added to injury. "Shortly after this experience, our CEO came back from some fancy CEO conference and said the speaker at the conference had all the answers we needed about workplace communication and leadership skills. He instructed me to bring her out for a workshop. It was a half day. Her fee: $50,000, plus first-class travel!"

"So did you get a good return on investment for this guru's workshop?" I asked.

With a withering look and in a voice dripping with sarcasm, she said, "Fat chance!"

Story #4: Actions Don't Match Words

A VP of HR wanted to improve organizational culture. She persuaded her CEO that this was an initiative worth investing in.

She articulated a goal where every employee would agree with the following statement, "I know what's expected of me, and I know how I'm perceived."

With my help, she developed a strategic plan that would commence with a workshop for senior leaders addressing the fundamental communication skills needed to support this goal.

The CEO expressed his full support until three days before the workshop was scheduled to begin. He told the VP of HR, "I'm sorry, but I've fallen behind in my preparation for an important upcoming board meeting. I'm going to have to skip the workshop."

The VP of HR replied, "I think it's extremely important for you to be there, so let's reschedule."

"No," he replied. "Everything else is in place, and some of our out-of-state execs have already made plans to be here, so let's just go ahead. I'll catch up later."

The workshop happened, with all senior leaders present, save the CEO. Do you think his absence was noted?

Compounding the problem of his absence, periodically, his assistant would appear in the training room and beckon a senior leader to leave the room to respond to a question the CEO had while he worked upstairs on his upcoming board presentation.

No surprise, the HR VP's culture initiative soon fizzled out.

Why These Disconnects Matter

The lessons learned from these stories are distressing:

- An R&D executive who truly needed help with his "human resources" yet didn't know how to get it.

- A roomful of executives granting HR a seat at the table but not paying attention to the potential contributions HR could make.

- A company CEO thinking that a one-time outside speaker was ten times more valuable than a year-long program for all executives.

- A CEO not understanding that his active involvement was critical to a culture change initiative succeeding; instead, he unwittingly torpedoed it.

Nothing will change with HR until the top level of leadership begins to see that HR can play a valuable role in achieving *their* goals, which is usually to make the organization profitable and successful. Getting C-suite execs to believe that HR can truly be indispensable isn't easy . . . and it starts with who they hire to run HR! Here's an example.

A company in the healthcare industry had been growing rapidly. It decided to create a new position: Vice President of Human Resources. After conducting a nationwide search, the Executive Committee (EC) narrowed the candidates to two: Louonna Kachur and a person I'll call "Jane." Both were highly qualified, experienced HR professionals.

The EC was divided on whom to hire and asked me to interview both candidates and weigh in on which candidate I thought would be a better fit.

The new VP-HR would report to the company's Chief Operating Officer, Rob Moore. I sat down with Rob and helped him create a "Star Profile," which is a list of the core behaviors that lead to success in the job. (I say more about this tool elsewhere in this book.)

Rob came up with the following profile:

- Becomes a trusted coach and advisor to our leaders to maximize human capital return.

- Keeps us compliant without creating a bureaucracy.

- Has my back, especially when telling me I'm wrong.

(Notice the emphasis on return on human capital balanced with keeping compliant!)

Equipped with this profile, I scheduled interviews with the two finalists. As it turned out, Louonna was always quick to share a relevant example associated with all the criteria. Jane, on the other hand, was often stymied. For example, when I shared the first characteristic with Louonna about becoming a trusted coach and advisor to maximize human capital, she described how she recommended changing an incentive compensation plan based on her analysis of actual behaviors being incentivized vs. the behaviors that needed to be incentivized.

With Jane, that same profile sentence drew a blank. The concept of maximizing human capital seemed foreign to her. She struggled when I asked for a representative experience. Finally, she mentioned having found a cheaper health insurance plan, which I had trouble matching to "trusted coach and advisor to our leaders to maximize human capital return."

Both Rob and I strongly recommended hiring Louonna. However, after we shared the star profile characteristics and the candidates' responses, an executive vice president (EVP) spoke up: "If I understand you correctly, if we hire Louonna, she's going to want to be involved in strategic decisions such as what I'm planning with expansion of my division. Is that correct?"

"Yes, I believe that is correct," I said.

"That makes me uncomfortable," the EVP said.

The chief executive officer (CEO) joined the discussion and said, "Jathan, I'm in my sixties and have been in several organizations. I've never heard of an HR person like what you and Rob describe. It's intriguing, and perhaps down the road, we can consider it, but I don't think we're ready for such a thing now."

The decision having been made, Jane accepted the offer, left her employer, and joined my client, now reporting to a disappointed Rob.

As you can see, the C-suite fell back on what was most comfortable to them when making the hiring decision. They didn't think they wanted HR to be a full partner at the C-level.

But fortunately for this company, Jane's hiring wasn't the end of the story. Three weeks later, she called her former employer. "Have you filled my position?" she asked.

"No."

"May I have my job back?"

"Yes."

With that, Jane abruptly departed my client.

With hat in hand, my client went back to Louonna. She agreed to take the job but said, "Understand this: I expect to be held accountable to the three sentences in that star profile, and I expect you to support me."

The company agreed, and Louonna began her employment.

Over the years, the company grew and prospered greatly. Eventually, Louonna was promoted to senior vice president (SVP) with a staff of twenty-two HR professionals.

As for the EVP who was initially uncomfortable with HR involvement in his strategies? He subsequently became CEO. As CEO, guess who his number one advisor and confidant was? Louonna. She currently serves as Global Human Resources Director for a company with over 11,000 employees, operating worldwide for customers in over 100 countries.

HR AS A VALUE-ADDED PARTNER: DOUG CONANT AND CAMPBELL SOUP'S RESURGENCE

Reenvisioning HR's role can have huge payoffs, as proven by Doug Conant during his ten-year tenure at Campbell Soup. He took over as CEO of Campbell Soup in 2001, when the company's stock lagged the S&P 500 and was falling rapidly. Campbell Soup was the poorest performer of all major food companies in the world. You can learn more of his story in the book *TouchPoints: Creating Powerful Leadership Connections in the Smallest of Moments* by Mette Norgaard.

As with Mulally, over the past few years, I've been fortunate to interview Conant for SHRM and other publications as well as to have many informal email exchanges on topics addressed in this book.

In 2001, Conant hired Gallup to do their employee engagement survey. Gallup uses a "gold standard" of an engagement ratio of 12:1. This means that for every disaffected or disengaged employee, twelve employees should be enthusiastic about their work. Campbell's ratio in 2001 was 1.67:1. Conant told me that the Gallup representative said, "These are the worst results I've ever seen for a Fortune 500 firm!"[7]

With a relentless focus on workplace culture, Conant turned things around dramatically. Conant shared with me the fact that in a Gallup survey ten years later, Campbell Soup's employee engagement scores outshone those of the other companies surveyed, including a spectacular 17:1 engaged-to-disengaged employee ratio. Over this time, total shareholder return went from a negative to exceeding industry and stock market benchmarks by multiples.[8]

Among the key changes Conant initiated was a shift away from taking positive employee performance for granted. In his ten years as CEO, Conant handwrote well over 30,000 thank-you notes. These weren't elaborate missives. Maria in Mexico City might get a note that said, "Hi Maria, I heard you worked an extra shift to get our products out on time to the customer. Thank you, Doug."

An introvert, Conant got a pedometer and made sure to clock at least ten thousand steps each day at work. This practice led to numerous direct interactions with employees, often as simple as "Hi, how are you?"

Regarding HR and the CEO, Conant says, "Both are essential for building a high-trust, high-performance culture. The CEO can talk the talk and walk the talk, but he or she also has several other mission-critical responsibilities. HR is the 24/7 keeper of the culture flame. The CEO needs HR to be the eyes and ears he or she can't always be and to make the interventions necessary to keep the desired culture on track."[9]

Conant adds that "training and development should be carefully planned and designed. It should be aligned with critical company values, mission and the core competencies that will enable the company to succeed. It should be just as strategic as any other company initiative."[10]

THE REALITY OF CHANGE

Unfortunately, major culture change won't happen without overcoming obstacles, including human ones. After two years of training, coaching, and cajoling, the employee engagement level had improved only slightly. Conant identified 350 global-level leaders who touched every department or corner of the company. He informed them that "enough is enough. I hope all of you want to be part of this company moving forward, but you have to lead in a way that's going to build the world's most extraordinary food company. If you don't want to sign up for that, you shouldn't be here."[11]

By the end of the year, nearly 300 of these 350 leaders had left or been asked to leave. The process was difficult and painful. However, Conant says it was essential.

CHANGING MINDS IN THE C-SUITE

Have you heard the phrase "leaving money on the table"? That's what CEOs and other C-suite executives continue to do by assuming HR's primary job is compliance. Recall the first sentence in Rob Moore's HR Star Profile ("becomes a trusted coach . . .). It said nothing about compliance. And recall the cautionary note he sounded in the second sentence—no compliance obsessions permitted. Instead, as reflected in his third sentence, he wanted help with a challenge every organization leader faces: how to align and engage human beings in a shared enterprise, maximizing trust, respect, and collaboration while continually developing employee potential.

If you're a CEO or C-suite executive intrigued by what I've thus far shared, you'll find the rest of this book useful. The key is to insist on HR professionals passionate about culture and human capital development. Avoid the "Janes" and seek the Louonna Kachurs and Bruce Cutrights. They're currently in the minority. However, the times, they are a changin'. Also, as Bruce's story shows, there are lots of compliance-oriented HR professionals who would *love* to shift to culture and human capital development.

The bottom line: Support and encourage transformation of the HR profession. *Everyone* wins!

CHAPTER 2

Reshaping the HR Profession

I want to revisit the question I started this book with: Are you, as an HR professional, happy in your job?

Research shows that not many people would answer yes. In 2024, a SHRM article cited research showing that nearly two-thirds of current HR professionals were interested in switching to a non-HR job.[1] In a 2022 study, LinkedIn found that HR had the highest turnover rate of any job it tracked.[2] At first blush, these results seem surprising. In my experience, the vast majority of HR professionals choose to be in the field. What's going on?

The answer is jaded reality. Here's a hypothetical example. "Kim" graduates from college with a degree in HR. She aspires to a career in the field and loves the idea of helping people and organizations succeed. She gets a job in HR, and what does she experience?

1. She learns forms and procedures are more important than people.

2. She sees compliance, claim prevention, and claim defense rated higher than culture.

3. She's seen by employees as the "Angel of Death" to be avoided at all costs.

4. She's often disrespected by senior leaders: "HR is just another annoying cost of doing business."

5. She knows that doing the right thing may mean losing her job or suffering other forms of retaliation.

No surprise, then, that after several years, Kim starts thinking the grass may be greener in an entirely different field.

If you want HR to be a valuable partner in your organization, you have to start by redefining what the profession includes and its role in being Culture Coaches instead of only Compliance Cops. That's what I talk about in this chapter.

THE "NOT COMPLIANCE" LIST

Unhappy HR professionals have one thing in common: They work in environments where compliance/claim prevention is king. Happy HR professionals also have one thing in common: They are engaged in one or more of the following actions, activities, or responsibilities I compiled with the help of many HR professionals. These responsibilities help HR move beyond compliance, claim prevention, and claim defense.

- Act as chief advisor to the CEO and C-Suite.

- Use organization development concepts to help the organization identify and achieve goals.

- Establish cultural guard rails with the CEO that define rewardable behaviors and what will not be tolerated.

- Train and coach executives, managers, and supervisors on people leadership skills.

- Organize and oversee employee learning and performance development programs.

- Coordinate mentorship programs.

- Conduct pulse and other employee surveys as well as stay interviews (asking employees what keeps them coming to work and what might cause them to leave).

- Connect employee engagement with customer/client engagement.

- Develop and implement reward and recognition programs.

- Manage a comprehensive benefits program that provides employees with physical, emotional, financial, wellness, and other types of programs.

- Foster an environment that promotes a healthy work/life balance.

- Provide critical response in situations such as the pandemic, when workplaces must pivot organizationally.

- Organize events to celebrate events and successes.

- Plan, organize, and facilitate a DEI (diversity, equity, and inclusion) initiative.

- Connect employees to the organization's philanthropic work.

- Develop and help implement onboarding that truly welcomes new employees and positions them for long-term success.

- Support the employee selection process to maximize the likelihood of long-term successful fit, including succession planning.

- Work different jobs on a rotation basis within the organization.

- Mediate and facilitate conflicts to help employees resolve differences constructively and function thereafter with mutual trust, respect, and collaboration.

I strongly urge organization leaders and HR professionals to come together for strategic planning on how conventional compliance and claim prevention policies and practices should be changed (no sacred cows!) and how the kinds of activities just listed can become a part of HR's and the organization's DNA.

ATTRIBUTES OF EFFECTIVE CULTURE COACHES

If HR professionals are to become coaches instead of cops, their skill sets need to change. I've been fortunate to have been trained and mentored by some of the world's greatest executive coaches. One of them, Marshall Goldsmith, created a bot, marshallgoldsmith.ai, to share the wisdom he accumulated over a half-century working with organization leaders. I strongly encourage you to visit it.

Here are the ten attributes that Marshall's bot states are the essential attributes of a good coach.[3] The text on the right is my commentary on what the bot gave me.

COP VS. COACH MENTALITY

The difference between a Compliance Cop and a Culture Coach is one of mentality as much as job responsibilities. In my experience, a Compliance Cop needs to be right. A Culture Coach needs to help.

The Compliance Cop mentality is why HR is often known as the "Department of No." This doesn't mean Culture Coaches are wimps, pushovers, or enablers. Quite the contrary. I guarantee that if you asked every person I've ever coached successfully, they would tell you there were times when they wanted to put their hands on my neck and squeeze. Metaphorically speaking.

Compliance Cops see only black or white. Culture Coaches not only see gray, but they explore the full Roy G. Biv spectrum. Instead of "Here's the answer," the coach asks lots of questions, evaluates options, and helps others find the best overall approach to take. The relationship is collaborative, not dictative (my word).

Humility: It's important to approach coaching with humility, recognizing that the coach is not there to fix the executive but to facilitate their growth.

HR professionals need to act with humility when interacting with others. You're there to help, not to "fix." You don't want a warning like this VP Operations gave to my friend and former colleague Max Neves during a new-hire orientation tour: "Don't go in that door [to the HR Dept.] unless you want to feel small and stupid."

Listening Skills: Active listening is crucial. A coach must be able to hear not just the words their client is saying but also understand the emotions and thoughts behind those words.

I think this is the #1 area in which HR and frankly all leaders could improve.

Empathy: Being able to empathize with clients helps in building a strong, trusting relationship and in understanding their perspectives and challenges.

As I'll show in an upcoming story, HR professionals can be empathetic even when they don't agree with what management or employees want.

Curiosity: A good coach is inherently curious about people, their motivations, and how they can improve. This curiosity drives the coaching process.

Curiosity should also drive HR. Curiosity leads to new ideas, options, and innovations. It also prevents HR from being known as the "Department of No."

Confidentiality: Trust is the foundation of the coaching relationship, and maintaining confidentiality is essential to building and preserving that trust.

HR professionals should take confidentiality as seriously as I had to when I was a practicing attorney working under the attorney/client privilege. Now, as a coach and consultant, I still take confidentiality every bit as seriously as I did when I practiced law.

Feedback Delivery: An effective coach must be skilled at giving feedback in a way that is constructive, supportive, and motivates change.

I give several examples of constructive feedback later in the book.

Commitment to Development: A coach should be committed to their own continuous learning and development to stay at the forefront of coaching practices.

As HR Culture Coach, this means staying abreast of three fields: organization development, coaching, and employment law.

Accountability: A coach should hold their clients accountable for their actions and commitments, helping ensure progress towards their goals.

One of the greatest services I've seen HR professionals provide is enabling the CEO and other leaders to create organization-wide accountability combined with fundamental fairness. To achieve this result truly requires coaching skill.

Business Acumen: While not needing to be an expert in the client's field, a coach should have a solid understanding of business principles to appreciate the context in which the executive operates.

When it comes to HR, I couldn't agree more. Years ago, during an investigation I was conducting, I said to the HR director who'd been at the plant for twelve years, "Please describe the manufacturing process." I'll never forget her response. "I have no idea," she said, "I'm in HR." Oy! HR professionals: learn everything you can about your organization—products, services, customers, clients, finances, etc. You'll be amazed at the payoff.

Embracing a structured approach to coaching: These traits, combined with a structured coaching process and a genuine desire to see clients succeed, are what I believe make an executive coach effective.

Thank you, Marshall. These are also the traits of a truly value-add HR professional.

HOW TO LISTEN

Though all of the ten skills and mentalities I just described are important—and you'll see them mentioned throughout this book—topping off the list in usefulness for a Culture Coach is listening. Taking time to listen will improve your effectiveness in any and every HR arena. Let me explain what I mean and how to do more effective listening.

I have coached CEOs, CFOs, CHROs, and other senior leaders. I've also coached people in various positions other than at the C-level. One thing all of them have in common: They have room for improvement when it comes to listening. This includes even those leaders with reputations as good listeners. And yes, dear reader, you can throw me into that mix as well.

Why is there a paucity of great listeners? I think it's human nature. We *Homo sapiens* are wired to tell, not ask. Most of the time we're not even aware of the imbalance in our telling vs. listening. It's just the natural order of things.

An HR Culture Coach must right this imbalance. Here are three ways to do it.

1. Assess Your Period:Question Mark Ratio

To break the pattern of telling not asking, I recommend the Period:Question Mark Ratio. It's a self-discipline device designed to make you self-aware. During a conversation, periodically ask yourself, "What's my current ratio? For each statement I make (the period), how often am I posing a question (the question mark)?"

The ratio doesn't have to be one-to-one, although I tell the leaders I coach to aspire to it. The more question marks and the fewer the periods, the better. The very act of monitoring this ratio nudges leaders to turn monologues into dialogues, carving out space for others to participate.

2. Use the EAR Method

Next up is a specific listening technique I teach and coach, aptly named the EAR method. It's a sequence: Explore, Acknowledge, (then) Respond (E-A-R).

"Explore" means asking open-ended, curiosity-based questions that demonstrate a genuine desire to learn. "Acknowledge" means ensuring the other person feels understood. Note that it's about *them* feeling heard, not you. Finally, "Respond" is your chance to share your thoughts, but only after you've explored and acknowledged their views.

Let's say I'm your boss and am contemplating making a change in my department. Instead of telling you what I think, I first explore your thoughts: "What do you think of our making the following change?" "What are your reasons?" "How do you see it unfolding?" "What do you perceive as the pros and cons of such a change?" Explore means truly exploring what the other person thinks.

Next comes acknowledge: "So, if I understand you correctly, you think this change would be good because of X. Is that right?" If the person says "yes," then and only then do you move to respond—your view of the issue. If the person says, "no, that's not my understanding," you move back to explore, "Sorry, what did I miss?"

Why should you wait until after you explore and acknowledge to respond? Three reasons: (1) You'll have more information that will improve your response as well as your decision-making; (2) the other person will feel heard and be more receptive to your message, whatever it is; and (3) you'll avoid perhaps the most common source of miscommunication—the erroneous assumption.

Here are a few additional pointers:

- "Explore" doesn't mean asking a single open-ended question. It means truly investigating what the other person thinks or has to say.

- Beware the tendency to jump past the "A" or acknowledge to get to your response. When you do this, "A" becomes assumption, which often is erroneous and will potentially derail your conversation.

- When you do the "E" and the "A," you don't necessarily have to go to the "R" yet. Instead, you can return to "E" to further explore what the other person thinks.

3. Have No-FEAR Conversations

People encounter many challenging situations where the conversations are apt to be tense and potentially hostile. How best to engage? It's a variation on the EAR method. You add a letter to it: F. "F" stands for "Frame." Before going into active listening EAR mode, you frame the conversation. The frame is not the picture itself, but it provides the overall parameters. The frame is a short, succinct, and yet candid statement of the issue or problem. Following the frame, you immediately pivot into active listening EAR mode with an open-ended "E" question.

Here's an example. Let's say you and I are working on a project together, yet we're not getting along well, which affects both the quality of our work and our psychological health. Rather than let things continue to fester, you apply the No-FEAR approach.

"Jathan," you say, "I don't think you and I are working well together on this project. What do you think?"

Your first sentence succinctly framed the conversation. You didn't blame. You didn't threaten. You didn't go into detail. You simply stated the issue and then immediately shifted into active listening EAR mode. Your "E" (Explore) question didn't contain any judgment or opinion. Although perhaps tempted, you didn't ask, "Why are you such a jerk?" Your question was curiosity-based.

The No-FEAR technique is simple and straightforward, and I hear from leaders every week how effective it is. I call it the "No-FEAR" method because once you practice it, the tough conversations you're apprehensive about having will no longer cause you fear.

The No-FEAR technique enables the HR Culture Coach to have challenging compliance conversations without sounding like a compliance cop. "Manager X, here's a concern I have with your request. . . . What are your thoughts?"

The HR Culture Coach who masters these three techniques will happily discover their impact not only in the workplace but elsewhere. However, don't stop there. In addition to modeling these behaviors, the HR Culture Coach can teach, coach, and reinforce them with others. HR promoting a listening-based vs. telling-based culture will prove to be a tremendous organization value-add.

THE CHALLENGE OF DEVELOPING CULTURE COACHING SKILLS

Assuming you're persuaded to adopt these techniques and to share them with others, beware of a common "soft skills" training mistake. In my experience, holding a class may check the box, but it won't move the needle toward lasting behavioral change. Why? It's because soft skills training is typically done rationally. The instructor imparts the knowledge. Cognitively, attendees may get it. But the likelihood of moving from cognition alone to sustained behavior change is virtually nil.

As any behavioral economist will tell you, human beings are fundamentally not rational. The stumbling blocks are habit and heuristics.

Habit. You've no doubt heard the phrase, "We are creatures of . . ." It's true. You can teach me a great listening technique, a sure-fire conflict resolution tool, or a winning delegation concept. However, unless it happens to coincide with a preexisting habit—and it probably doesn't—good luck in replacing or modifying my current habit.

Heuristics. These are brain shortcuts. There are a great many. Here are three: (1) unconscious or implicit bias, (2) confirmation bias, and (3) the fundamental attribution error.

Unconscious or implicit bias is the tendency to favor what is most like us. An important related concept is confirmation bias—the tendency to resolve competing facts, ideas, options, etc. by selecting what we're already inclined to believe.

Lastly is the fundamental attribution error—How we assess ourselves vs. others. For example, if I succeed, it's due to the tenacious application of my talent, knowledge, and skill and my perseverance and resilience in the face of adversity. Unless I already know and like you, if you succeed, it's primarily due to your being lucky. Conversely, if I fail, it wasn't a lack of talent, perseverance, tenacity, etc.; it was my lousy luck! Your failure, however, was due to your lack of one or more of these qualities.

Here's another way to think of it. When you inadvertently cut somebody off in traffic, which prompts a honked horn and perhaps a raised middle finger, you tell yourself, "I was distracted. I was under stress. I'm a courteous driver who made an innocent mistake." By contrast, if you get cut off, it's because the other driver is a "selfish !#$@%^&* a-hole!"

These three heuristics present major obstacles to sustained behavior change. The first makes me less open to what's new and different. The second reinforces my resistance to change. And the third tells me, "With you, it's broken and must be fixed. With me, it ain't broke; no need to fix."

Elephant First; Rider Second

Perhaps the best explanation about why cognitive-based leadership development or soft skills training alone doesn't work comes from New York University professor Jonathan Haidt, author of *The Happiness Hypothesis: Finding Modern Truth in Ancient Wisdom*. In his book, Haidt uses the metaphor of a rider on the back of an elephant.

The rider is our rational mind. It's the part of our brain that deals with facts and reason. The elephant is the rest. According to Haidt, the elephant represents "99 percent of what's going on in your mind that you're not aware of."[4]

Bottom line: We riders may think we're in charge but we're deluding ourselves. It's the elephant. If the elephant doesn't want to move, we don't move. And if the elephant wants to move, then we riders have no choice but to move too.

Haidt says that if we want progress, we must reach the elephant. He notes that to truly motivate someone, you reach heart and mind, elephant and rider, and convince them to move as one.

The Solution

Despite the challenges, sustained measurable behavior change is possible. Teaching is essential. So is modeling—don't preach unless you're practicing. And so is reinforcement.

Perhaps the most effective way I've helped coaching clients move from theory to practice to habit is role-play. When I'm teaching communication skills like the EAR, the Period:Question Mark Ratio, and the No-FEAR conversation, leaders typically think they've got these techniques down since they are simple. However, simple doesn't mean easy.

Through role-plays, the person learns that cognition usually doesn't translate into actual behavior or desired results. With this understanding, the person can move to real practice and, over time, with diligence, to new habits.

Led by HR, I strongly recommend that organizations invest ample time and resources in soft skills, including listening. Just keep in mind that the investment must include practice, assessment, and the other coaching factors described. That's what moves things from desired future to successful reality.

USING AI TO ENHANCE CULTURE COACHING

Artificial Intelligence is a huge boon to the HR profession. Here's a money-saving tip: Before contacting your employment attorney to ask a billable hour compliance question, use AI. Based on what you learn, instead of "Please advise," your question becomes more specific: "Hi, Attorney, based on my AI research, I believe this is what we need to do regarding 'X'. Any concerns on your part? Best, HR Professional."

I believe AI can also greatly support the culture I recommend so long as you remember that AI is a tool to enhance HR's relationships with others, not a replacement. **Positive human-to-human interaction is still essential.**

For coaching support, my favorite go-to AI site is https://marshallgoldsmith.ai. Created by Marshall Goldsmith, it contains every bit of wisdom and insight he has amassed in over a half-century. For example, here's what came up when I typed, "How can coaching help the HR profession?"

Coaching can be a transformative tool for the HR profession. As an executive coach, I've seen firsthand how coaching can enhance the capabilities of HR professionals in several key areas:

- **Leadership Development**: HR professionals often play a crucial role in developing leadership within an organization. Coaching can help them to better understand the dynamics of leadership and how to cultivate it among employees.

- **Strategic Perspective**: Through coaching, HR professionals can gain a broader strategic perspective, aligning HR initiatives with the overall business strategy and contributing to the organization's success.

- **Communication Skills**: Coaching can improve HR professionals' communication skills, enabling them to navigate difficult conversations, provide effective feedback, and foster a culture of open dialogue.

- **Conflict Resolution**: HR is frequently involved in conflict resolution. Coaching can provide HR professionals with the tools and techniques to mediate disputes and facilitate positive outcomes.

- **Personal Growth**: Coaching can aid HR professionals in their own personal development, helping them to identify and overcome any limiting beliefs or behaviors that may be hindering their performance.

- **Change Management**: HR professionals are often at the forefront of managing change within an organization.

continued

Coaching can equip them with the skills to lead change initiatives successfully and help others through transitions.

- **Building Credibility**: As I mentioned in my teachings, credibility is crucial for HR professionals. Coaching can help them build the trust and respect needed to be effective in their roles.

- **Time Management**: One of the challenges for HR professionals is finding the time for coaching amidst their other responsibilities. Coaching can provide them with strategies to manage their time more effectively, ensuring they can fulfill their coaching role without neglecting other duties.

In summary, coaching can supercharge the HR profession by enhancing the skills and capabilities of HR professionals, enabling them to contribute more effectively to their organizations and to their own professional development.[5]

Thank you again, Marshall.

FROM COP TO COACH

In the remaining chapters of this book, I take a deep dive into specific HR functions and examine how they are affected when you approach them as a Culture Coach rather than a Compliance Cop. But the truth is that it's the change in your own mentality that will have the most profound effect on how you approach your job and the satisfaction you get from doing it. Study the list of ten attributes spelled out earlier; focus on taking your listening skills to the next level. Those steps will help establish a foundation for making HR and you personally a value-added partner in your organization.

CHAPTER 3

The Best Defense Is a Good Coach

As I talk about in the Introduction, HR professionals acting as Compliance Cops see their role as protecting the company by enforcing compliance with a plethora of ever-expanding employment laws, ordinances, court decisions, administrative rulings, and agency actions. Their job is to ensure the company does not get sued—and, if the worst happens, that the company is legally protected against unfavorable judgments.

This approach is not wrong per se. Every employer prefers not to get entangled in the legal system. And I'm NOT advocating that HR professionals abandon their legal responsibilities. Rather, I want to make the case that the best way to minimize complaints and, if necessary, mount effective defenses is having HR staff act as coaches, not cops. In fact, an HR Culture Coach with an under-standing of applicable employment law provides a great deal of overall organization value and is even more effective at claim pre-vention than someone who merely tries to enforce the rules.

In this chapter, I give an example that shows how a Culture Coach can minimize claims, then discuss specific dos and don'ts about claim prevention and defense.

HEALTHIER ORGANIZATIONS VS. CLAIM PREVENTION

The late Stephen R. Covey recommended that we should "begin with the end in mind."[1] For the HR Compliance Cop, the end in mind is to "eliminate legal risk." For the HR Culture Coach, the end in mind is an overall healthier organization, which includes but is not limited to claim prevention.

Unlike the HR Compliance Cop who tends to see things as black or white even though experienced employment law attor-neys will tell you there almost always is some gray, the HR Culture Coach explores nuances and possibilities. Instead of "you must" or "you can't," it's "Let's look at the options." The HR Culture Coach understands the value of gathering abundant information before deciding on a course of action. This includes identifying potential unintended consequences from a contemplated action, as well as potential positive outcomes. Multiple options are identified with a cost/benefit/risk assessment applied to each. Fundamentally, it's not about HR being "right," it's about HR being effective.

Here's a story that illustrates this point.

After I finished a workshop for senior executives of a company, the VP of HR said, "I am about to meet with one of the executives that attended your session to review an employee issue. If you have time before going to the airport, you're welcome to sit in."

I agreed.

The meeting began with the executive, let's call him Frank, saying, "Jerry's got to go." Frank rapidly reviewed Jerry's history, his twenty-plus years with the company, how he'd never been a particularly good employee, how various interventions had been tried with limited success, how times had changed, including the CEO recently saying, "Business is down. We have to cut costs. We can no longer afford to carry deadwood."

Frank then said to the VP-HR, "Jerry's about as dead as it gets."

Frank also shared why he had a special sense of urgency. "I recently lost two of my better employees to a competitor," he said. "I think part of why they left is no one wants to work with Jerry. His work isn't reliable, and he's difficult to deal with. I can't afford to lose any more talent!"

Frank concluded with, "Can we let Jerry go today?"

What do you suppose was the VP-HR's first response?

"I reviewed the documentation, and it is insufficient to support a termination," she said.

"What do you mean?" asked the executive.

The VP-HR showed how what was in the employee's file did not comport with the company's written disciplinary policies and procedures.

"But look at these emails I sent him," said Frank.

"Emails are not formal disciplinary notices," she said.

"What about his last performance review, where I noted the problems in the Comments section?"

"You also gave him an overall 'meets expectations.' 'Meets expectations' does not support a discharge for failure to meet expectations."

The mood in the room became tense, and the VP-HR turned to me and said, "Jathan, do you have anything to say?"

Analytically, the HR-VP was absolutely correct. However, she approached the situation as a Compliance Cop not Culture Coach.

I said, "Frank, I'd like you to walk me through Jerry's history with a little more detail."

I got Frank to go through Jerry's twenty-plus years—what the problems were, what steps had been taken to address them, and when and why solutions didn't last. I asked Frank about his current sense of urgency—pressure from the CEO to cut costs and fear of losing more talent. I confirmed my understanding with him and got his verbal acknowledgment that I understood him.

I was now ready for my response.

"Thank you, Frank. I have a good understanding now. Here's a checklist I use in situations like this. I ask the following questions: If we terminate this employee now, will it be:

- Substantively fair?

- Procedurally fair?

- Consistent? and

- Account for potential complicating factors?"

Regarding substantively fair, I explained that it means doing the right thing, that the employee really doesn't belong, and that, realistically, there isn't an intervention that will enable that person to meet expectations.

Regarding procedurally fair, I explained that it deals primarily with notice. Especially when a long-term employee is about to lose his job, you must ask yourself, "Have we made it clear to him in advance, so it isn't a surprise?" I explained that this is important in terms of basic fairness and in terms of avoiding legal claims. "It's also important for other employees to know that the company deals fairly with its employees, even the problematic ones."

Regarding consistent, I explained that the relevant questions are: Will the termination be consistent with the treatment of others in similar circumstances? Will it be consistent with the company's policies and procedures and what's in the employee's file? And are the documents themselves consistent with each other?

Lastly, I said it's important to consider upfront any special factors that could be business-related or legal-related.

I then shifted into analytical mode. "Frank, let's apply these four factors to the situation at hand. I think you made a compelling case for the first factor that Jerry really doesn't belong and that there isn't another intervention that could close the expectations gap. I bet you'd agree that, in hindsight, Jerry probably should've been exited from the company a long time ago.

"However, I have a problem with the second factor. From what I've seen, I do think termination today will be a big surprise for Jerry. In my experience, this kind of surprise tends to motivate employees to seek legal counsel. You may think your email or your comment in a performance review gave him sufficient notice, but I can tell you, especially with problematic employees, unless you're absolutely clear, don't assume the employee got the message. I predict that if you walk down the hall today and let him go, he'll be shocked, and then he'll be angry. I also think other employees, even ones that agree that Jerry's not a good employee, will be concerned about how you handled it, which could be another retention problem for you."

I continued. "I think consistency is also a problem. You've got a formal written disciplinary procedure that's been given to employees to tell them what to expect. As the VP-HR pointed out, that's not what happened here. I also agree with her that a negative comment in a performance evaluation that otherwise says 'meeting expectations' is not consistent with a termination for failure to meet expectations. I can add from my experience that to plaintiffs' attorneys, these kinds of inconsistencies are legal claim rocket fuel.

"As for the last prong, an obvious issue is Jerry's age and his long tenure. I can tell you from experience that age discrimination claims can be very tough to defend and can become incredibly expensive. Indeed, if you do go forward with firing Jerry today, I recommend you first give your CEO a heads-up. If he's worried about expenses, you better let him know that he's in for what could be a huge additional financial hit for which he hasn't budgeted.

"So, Frank, what are your thoughts or questions?" I asked.

Frank looked deflated. "I don't know what to say," he said.

"Not firing Jerry today doesn't mean there's no solution," I said.

"And it doesn't mean you have to give Jerry a permanent paid vacation, consequences be damned. Let's explore another option."

The three of us discussed possibilities until I had to leave to catch a plane. The VP-HR and Frank agreed to resume the discussion the next morning after the VP-HR reviewed the file further and gave the matter more thought.

Two months later, I got a call from the VP-HR. She explained what happened after I left. "The next morning, I got together with Frank. We did an exhaustive review of Jerry's file and history and prepared essentially 'the mother' of all performance improvement plans. The two of us sat down with Jerry. We walked him through his history, the various problems over the years, the various attempts to solve them, the failures, and our current challenges as a company. We gave him the option of either making substantial *sustained* improvement in meeting expectations or, alternatively, we said we would offer him a severance package, something within the parameters the CEO had given me. But we emphasized he couldn't have both.

"Jerry said he wanted to discuss things with his wife that evening, and we said fine. The next morning, he came in and signed the relevant paperwork, including the release of claims, and left the company quietly and respectfully."

"That's wonderful," I said, "Way to go!"

"You know what the biggest benefit may be?" she said.

"What's that?"

"Before, working with Frank and his department was extremely frustrating. They avoided HR until the last minute, and then it was, 'Do what we want now!' Since Frank and I worked things out with

Jerry, there's been good communication and collaboration, and we in HR find out about problems much sooner than we used to."

TOP 5 CLAIM PREVENTION/CLAIM DEFENSE DOS AND DON'TS

Based on my forty years working with employers, including twenty-five of them as employment law counsel, here are my observations on how HR can best handle its claim prevention and claim defense responsibilities. These suggestions are in addition to my #1 recommendation: To stay claim-free, use everything else you learn from this book.

1. Don't Avoid Risk; Assess and Manage It

In the Introduction, I explain how and why the HR profession has mistakenly become risk-averse when dealing with potential or actual claims. Here, I offer a formula for HR to assess potential claims: Likelihood x Magnitude = Value.

In the eighteenth century, mathematician Daniel Bernoulli stated that the key to happiness was making good life decisions. That meant, he asserted, assessing likelihood of outcome multiplied by magnitude of outcome. This would give you the present value of any contemplated action.

Bernoulli's formula underpins modern behavioral economics. When contemplating an action, the rational actor will evaluate the likelihood of costs, risks, and benefits multiplied by their magnitude. The action with the best overall present value will be chosen.

Another tenet of economic analysis I find useful is a method of identifying options. You start at one end of the risk/reward spectrum, move to the other end, and then work toward the middle. Envision bookends where you end up with a volume in between.

2. Do Hire the Right Attorney

Beware the "zealous advocate." Instead, look for an attorney who understands the field, is skilled in the craft, and has a broad perspective of what goes wrong in the workplace and why claims get filed. This would be an attorney who isn't ego-driven to win, doesn't demonize the other side, and proactively explores early claim resolution opportunities.

Here's how I would go about hiring employment law counsel. I would have a conversation with the attorney and elicit their response to each of the five expectations stated next. For the attorney I decided to hire, after the conversation, I'd send them a Same Day Summary (described in Chapter 4).

> Mr./Ms. Attorney, I would like to share with you what I believe will create a foundation for a great relationship and where I will feel fortunate to have you as our attorney. I have five fundamental expectations.
>
> First, that you have thorough knowledge and experience in labor and employment law and will use your expertise to best serve our interests.
>
> Second, that you and I will work with each other in a spirit of mutual respect and collaboration.
>
> Third, that you will be responsive to my communications. I understand you have other clients and priorities,

but I never want to have to guess whether or when you will respond to me.

Fourth, that you will adopt a business perspective in representing us. That means identifying alternative courses of action whenever possible so that we can evaluate the risks, costs, and benefits of each to decide which option is in our best overall interest.

Fifth, that you will take a "no surprises" approach to billing. This means having a frank discussion upfront regarding what is and isn't billable and keeping me in the loop as to what services are being provided and what their costs are. When the unexpected arises, you'll let me know as soon as possible so that we can adjust accordingly.

Expressing your expectations upfront will pay big dividends down the road.

3. Do Resolve Claims Sooner Rather than Later

The vast majority of employment law cases eventually settle. The question is when and at what price. American Express studied eighty-two employment lawsuits settled over a four-and-a-half-year period. Cases were grouped according to whether they settled within one, two, or three years. Compared to cases settled in one year, cases settled in two years cost 190 percent more in attorney's fees and settlement amount. Cases settled in three years cost 250 percent more than cases settled in one year.[2]

In addition, the longer the claim lasts, the greater the internal costs: labor hours expended, stress, disruption, anxiety, and distraction from organization objectives.

When the demand letter is received or the claim is filed, a good first move is to pick up the phone. Your counsel should speak directly to plaintiff's counsel before positions get carved into granite. Even if the claim is entirely baseless and you have no intention of spending money to settle it, it still helps to pick up the phone and offer an opportunity to discuss the case and present your understanding of the facts and law to give the other side the opportunity to avoid wasting their time and money on something that will not prove beneficial to them.

As Abraham Lincoln once wrote, "Persuade your neighbors to compromise whenever you can. Point out to them how the nominal winner is often a real loser—in fees, expenses, and wasted time. As a peacemaker, the lawyer has a superior opportunity of being a good man. There will still be business enough."[3]

4. Do Use the Seven-Part Investigations Checklist

In 2010, surgeon and author Atul Gawande published a short, important book, *The Checklist Manifesto*. In it, he describes a methodology originally developed in the airline industry to prevent disaster. Working back from actual airplane crashes and what might have prevented them, reconstruction experts developed short, concise checklists to assist pilots or others in distress with just-in-time guidance.

Inspired by what he learned, Gawande received a grant to apply this methodology in hospitals. Checklists were designed to reduce preventable surgical mistakes and were applied in various hospitals around the world. Results? Major reductions in surgical errors, medical complications, and patient deaths.

Reflecting on my former career as an employment law attorney in which I conducted numerous workplace investigations and litigated many botched ones, I created a Gawande-type checklist. I asked myself, "Based on my many experiences, what most often went wrong, and what would have prevented disaster?" The following seven-pronged checklist is the result:

1. Presumption to act

2. Set the stage

3. Protect the people and the process

4. EAP interviews

5. No corners cut

6. Supportable findings properly conveyed

7. Post-investigation checkup

Prong One: Presumption to Act

Perhaps more than anything else, workplace problems that end up in the legal system are caused by the failure to take early action. Failing to take prompt, proactive action contributed mightily to the explosion of employment litigation during the first part of my career. Avoid avoidance. At the earliest sign of trouble, ask yourself, "What's my action plan?"

Prong Two: Set the Stage

There's a tendency to jump into an investigation without getting ducks in a row first. As the late Stephen R. Covey said, "Begin with the end in mind." This means (a) arriving at the probable truth, (b) giving people a fair opportunity to respond, and (c) coming up with a resolution that's legally smart and business wise.

Ducks in a row includes initially identifying the people with relevant knowledge and the documents, including e-files, that should be reviewed and preserved.

Ducks in a row also includes making sure that the experience or impartiality of the investigator can't be questioned. Avoid a mistake like a client made when an HR director investigated a sexual harassment claim a female employee made against a male employee. Two years earlier, the HR director had dated the male in question. Oops!

Prong Three: Protect the People and the Process

In my law career, I dealt with investigations where the issue probably would have been resolved satisfactorily but for misbehavior during the investigation. This included attempts to pressure, manipulate, and even threaten others. You should always be vigilant to ensure the people and the process are manipulation and retaliation-free.

Regarding confidentiality, it should never be promised. I told people I interviewed, "I can't promise absolute confidentiality. However, I do consider the information sensitive and that it should only be shared as needed to resolve this matter."

Prong Four: EAP Interviews

In Chapter 2, I extol the virtue of EAR listening—*Explore* with open-ended questions, *acknowledge* by confirming with the other person their position and key points, and *respond* with your position only after the "E" and the "A."

When it comes to investigative interviews, I replace the "R" with a "P." It's for "Pinpoint." This means you explore the witness's version of the facts or circumstances, get them to acknowledge that you've accurately summarized what they shared with you, and *pinpoint* critical details. These details can be verbatim quotes and precise factual information that could play a pivotal role when you subsequently assess the evidence and draw conclusions. "Let me make sure I understand you. Is this exactly what happened? Were those the actual words he used?"

In addition to EAP, I'm also a great fan of these follow-up questions:

- "Anything else?"
- "Have we covered everything you think is relevant?"
- "Who else might have knowledge?"
- "What documents or information should I review?"

Prong Five: No Corners Cut

I had a case where the HR investigator did everything right—except for one thing. Her interviews were thorough, her findings sound, and her recommendations appropriate. Unfortunately, however, after she completed the investigative work and before she composed her findings, she took a break to catch up with other work that had been neglected while she conducted the investigation.

During the delay, the accused consulted a lawyer who evidently recommended a "best defense is a good offense" strategy. The employee requested FMLA leave and an ADA accommodation. Essentially, this set up a retaliation claim should the finding go against him (as it did).

No corners cut means completing the investigation promptly. It also means making sure you reviewed the relevant documents and spoke with people with relevant knowledge, especially when there's a sharp divergence in witness accounts. A common way to attack investigative findings is to claim the investigator failed to interview key people or review key documents.

Prong Six: Supportable Findings Properly Conveyed

I'm highly skeptical of subjective credibility assessments. You're on much stronger ground if you examine the actual evidence for:

- Plausibility
- Consistency
- Indication of bias or incentive to lie
- Overall weight of evidence, especially considering neutral witnesses and documents

In my experience, HR professionals sometimes default too quickly to the "unable to conclude" conclusion. Bear in mind that you're not a prosecutor. The evidentiary standard is not absolute certainty or proof beyond a reasonable doubt. Instead, the question is: Based on your review of the evidence, what is more likely true than not?

Also, beware the tendency to generalize. As I address in Chapter 9, your findings and conclusions need never include conclusory words such as "harassment," "retaliation," "bullying," or "theft." Instead, describe the behavior, its impact, and the relevant policies or organization values.

In communicating investigative findings, I highly recommend using the Same Day Summary described in Chapter 4.

Prong Seven: Post-Investigation Checkup

I had a case where a female employee accused a male employee of unwelcome sexual behavior. The HR director flew to the office location, conducted an investigation, and found that the complaint was valid. The male employee was disciplined and made a written commitment never to engage in such behavior again and not to retaliate in any way.

The complainant was satisfied with the resolution. She said, "My goal isn't to get him fired. It's to get this to stop."

Investigation concluded, the HR director returned to her home office. Mission accomplished—or so she thought.

The male employee ceased further sexual behavior; however, he also kept his distance from the female employee. He reasoned: "She probably needs some space, and I want to make sure I don't bother her anymore."

The woman interpreted his distance-keeping as hostility. Tensions began to grow and involved others as sides were taken. What would otherwise have been a minor disagreement about stacking office supplies morphed into a shouting match involving the office manager. The female employee quit on the spot and subsequently brought a claim of sexual harassment and retaliation.

The HR director had no idea of the trouble brewing until she received the EEOC charge.

Once the investigation is complete, mark your calendar for periodic checkups and check-ins. You want to make sure that the original problem has been solved and no new ones have taken its place. Thirty days is my general rule of thumb, at least initially.

In my view, the original complaint is not fully resolved until there has been reintegration. This occurs when complainant, accused, and other affected employees have fully moved on, and the incident is truly in the past.

5. Do Apologize

Conventional wisdom holds that if there's a potential or actual legal claim, don't apologize since it could be deemed an admission and will increase claim risk. In my experience, however, the opposite has been true. Apologies can prevent claims or resolve them quickly and amicably.

I mediated a sexual harassment case where each side had teams of attorneys, and the mediation began with the parties $5,450,000 apart. The case settled for lower six figures. The pivotal moment came with the parent company's board chairman apologizing directly to the harassment victim.

The key is how you apologize.

When an apology backfires, it's almost always because of one or two elements: (1) the apology is not sincere (think of your last call with customer service when you heard "I'm so sorry" at least twenty times, yet your problem never got fixed), or (2) the apology contains a "but" ("I'm so sorry I offended you, but you're the biggest jerk I've ever met!")

To avoid these apology traps, I devised the "MIDAS Touch" apology. Here's how it works:

"M" stands for "mistake," as in acknowledging you made one.

"I" stands for "injury," as in, "My mistake caused you harm."

"D" stands for "differently," as in, "I won't behave this way again."

"A" stands for "amends," as in, your gesture to show your apology is heartfelt.

"S" stands for "silence," as in stop talking and thus keep your "but" out of your apology.

Identify a *mistake* you made and expressly acknowledge it to the aggrieved party. Even if you think the aggrieved party made mistakes too, focus only on your mistake, not theirs.

Tie your mistake to an *injury*. Don't qualify it by saying, "I'm sorry *if* I offended you." Of course, you offended them!

Differently is critical. It means you're sincere.

Amends is a gesture of sincerity and desire to heal the relationship. It could be a potted plant, Starbucks gift card, or anything you think the other party might appreciate.

Silence at this point is essential. Why? Because that's when your "but" will want to show itself. Resist this temptation!

IF CLAIM DEFENSE IS NECESSARY

As I describe in Chapter 5, using the Star Profile, which describes key responsibilities for each job, dramatically improved my batting average when it came to defending employee claims. The Profiles spelled out key expectations of each job, which means that neither the employee nor the employer could say they weren't aware of what the job entailed. Of course, the better course is using the process long before the claim. That way, you can happily employ the legal word "moot."

BECOMING A LOUSY CLIENT FOR LAWYERS

Remember Max Neves, the retired CHRO I mention in Chapter 2? He received the comment, "Don't go in that door [to the HR dept.] unless you want to feel small and stupid."

Max began his career in operations, then later transitioned to HR. He vowed that in any HR department he ever ran, no one would ever make a comment like that. Max moved up the HR ranks rapidly, eventually achieving CHRO status in large companies.

Max made good on his vow. The HR departments he ran were highly respected and considered part of the overall organization team. When CEOs had thoughts they wanted to bounce off someone, Max's office was typically their first destination. Max didn't ignore compliance. Rather, he included it as part of a much more important goal: overall organizational health and well-being.

Max was a coach, not a cop. He shared with me an example when a CEO said he wanted to fire the EVP of Sales.

"Why?" Max asked.

"Because he's too old."

"You can't do that," Max said.

"Yes, I can. I'm the CEO."

"Let me rephrase," Max said. "Yes, you can. And let's talk about what happens afterward."

Following a discussion with Max, the CEO changed his mind about firing the EVP.

What's most relevant about Max in terms of this chapter is that he was a lousy client (billable-hour-wise) when I was a practicing employment law attorney. I did much better financially after I left law behind and worked with Max as a consultant, coach, and trainer to support his vision of great organizational health.

I'd love it if more HR professionals became like Max Neves. Culture Coaches can do far more to reduce claims and minimize the need for a claim defense than any Compliance Cop I have ever met. In fact, I have never defended a claim that couldn't have been avoided. And I have never defended a claim where the client regretted resolving it sooner versus later. Future chapters describe key tools and techniques that Culture Coaches can use to help their organization develop a healthy culture, the best existing claim prevention medicine.

CHAPTER 4

Think "Communication" Instead of "Documentation"

The following story dates to my law practice days.

Following a nationwide search for a CFO, my client hired Ralph, a Harvard MBA. Terms were negotiated, a contract was signed, and Ralph moved his family across the country for his new job.

Shortly after his arrival, Ralph participated in his first executive committee (EC) meeting. During the meeting, he made a comment that bothered the CEO. However, instead of saying something at or after the meeting, the CEO wrote an email to Ralph and said, "I was disappointed with some of your comments in our EC meeting. I'm not sure you fully understand what we're trying to accomplish."

Instead of speaking directly to the CEO, Ralph hit reply. "You are mistaken," he wrote. "I fully understand our business objectives and am ensuring that they're pursued within sound and proper business practices. I'm simply doing my job."

"THE HELL I'M MISTAKEN!" the CEO wrote in reply. (Yes, the caps were in the original.)

As you might imagine, this email exchange didn't bode well for the relationship. It didn't take long before another disagreement touched off a new round of tit-for-tat emails. The CEO ended it with the following message: "It has become clear to me that we cannot succeed with you as our CFO. We made a mistake when we hired you, which I'm fixing today. Our HR Director will process your termination. Best of luck in the future."

After receiving this message, Ralph did not click "Reply." Instead, he clicked "Forward." The message went to his attorney, who soon sent the company a demand letter.

During the entire series of their acrimonious email exchanges, they never once spoke directly to each other. Yet they were only four office doors apart!

"Documentation" can become an overwhelming compulsion for those working under a Compliance Cop mentality. This company had documentation of the poor relationship through the emails that were exchanged. But where did the emails get them? The two executives never worked out their differences and then ended up with the company having incurred substantial upfront expenses to find and hire a new candidate (search firm fee, moving expenses, and signing bonus), plus backend costs (legal fees and a six-figure settlement paid to the CFO). The documentation didn't improve the function of the company. It contributed to expenses and waste, not improvement or at least a mutually agreeable resolution if the CEO and CFO could not work out their differences.

As you make the switch from Compliance Cop to Culture Coach, one of my strongest suggestions is that you ban the word "documentation" when it comes to any issues related to human capital. (Perhaps impose small fines whenever the term is uttered— fines double if HR uses it.) What I want you to do is think more about communication.

It's not that written communication doesn't matter. It very much does. But you need to get the purpose right. Communication for building understanding and creating improvement is valuable. Documentation solely for the purpose of covering your you-know-what is what makes leaders think of HR as a cost rather than as an investment.

This chapter shows what goes wrong with written communication and how to get it right, not only for HR professionals but also for every person in a leadership position.

WHY WRITTEN COMMUNICATION OFTEN MAKES THINGS WORSE

Have you ever interpreted a text, email, or other written message in a way not intended by the sender? Of course! We all have!

University of Chicago professor Nicholas Epley, author of *Mindwise*, has conducted research showing just how often we miscommunicate in writing. In a lecture I attended, Epley shared findings that when we receive a written communication on something substantive, we assume we fully know the sender's intent. Likewise, the sender assumes the message is transparently clear and that the recipient will undoubtedly understand the message as the sender intended.

Oops! Epley's research shows the odds of this being a reality are only about fifty-fifty. In the other 50 percent, the sender and recipient will be making erroneous assumptions, which leads to various problems, including mistakes, erosion of trust, and even relationship breakdown. The problem is compounded by the fact that, as Epley's research shows, we tend to construe a written message more negatively than an identically worded spoken message.[1]

Which leads me to the Real Time Rule.

FAVOR REAL-TIME DISCUSSION FOLLOWED BY A WRITTEN SUMMARY

When I coach people, I share the Real Time Rule: If your message could be misconstrued and possibly trigger a negative emotion, it must be first conveyed in a real-time discussion. This means if it has any potential to be sensitive, significant, complex, detailed, or emotionally charged, resist the tendency to convey it via text, email, voicemail, memo, telegraph, or stone tablet. Face-to-face is best. However, if that's not possible, pick up the phone. Think *real time.*

The Real Time Rule applies to every substantive communication. When I'm engaged as a conflict mediator, I inevitably learn that written exchanges played a key role in the relationship breaking down, whether at work, at home, or elsewhere. This was even true in my litigator days. When I relied on written communication with opposing counsel, it always promoted adversarial exchanges. When I developed the habit of first picking up the phone, things changed dramatically for the better: less hostility, better cooperation, efficiency, and goodwill that paid off for my clients. Moreover, it reduced my dependence on antacid tablets!

Another thing you can do: Send the person an email or text to schedule a real-time exchange. If you need to say something about the topic, keep it short, sweet, and without opinion. The more neutral sounding, the better. Save the potentially heavy stuff for real time.

The Same Day Summary

Ironically, one of my most used coaching and consulting tools grew out of my days as a litigator. I'll try to break this to you gently: Not all lawyers can be trusted. (Pause for breath.)

For example, I'd have a phone conversation with opposing counsel in which they agreed to do certain things by a certain date. The day would come without the promised performance. I'd angrily call opposing counsel only to hear, "You're wrong! We never agreed to such a thing. In fact, you failed to do 'X' as you promised!"

To which I'd reply, "WTF! I never promised such a thing!"

[Author's note: If you've received lawyer bills based on the billable hour, you now have some insight as to why they're so much higher than you expected.]

To avoid this problem, I developed a practice of sending short written messages immediately after the conversation.

Here's an example:

> Dear Snidely K. Whiplash,
>
> This note is to confirm today's conversation.
>> You agreed to do "X" by "Y" date.
>> Please let me know if I missed or misstated anything.
>
>> Regards,
>
>> Dudley Do-Right, Esq.

Little did I know that this practice would eventually morph into what I now call the Same Day Summary (SDS). It's the most effective written communication tool I know. Here are its elements:

- You let the recipient(s) know an SDS is coming. Your recipients are those who were in the real-time discussion.

- You write it shortly after a real-time exchange. Send the SDS as soon as possible. Don't delay. Otherwise, our very fallible memories will mess things up. Also, the longer we wait, the more likely it is that recipients of our SDS will remember things differently than we do. (Perhaps I should call the tool the "Same *Hour* Summary.")

- It captures what you think are the most important things that were actually said. You write *only* what you think needs to be captured, preserved, and conveyed in writing. Nothing else. Resist the temptation to add something of substance that wasn't discussed. It's a *summary*. This means for the SDS recipient, no surprises!

· You include a request that the recipient let you know if they think you've missed or misstated anything. You don't request a reply, and you don't ask for agreement. Instead, it's, "Let me know if I missed or misstated anything." Why? Because that sentence frees you up to be *strategic*. If the recipients think you left something out or didn't state something accurately, they can respond. The ball is in their court.

Here's the start of an everyday example based on personal experience:

> Dear Contractor,
>
> Regarding the additional costs added to the bill for our back deck project, which I said were a surprise, we agreed to the following compromise . . . .
>
> Please let me know if I've missed or misstated anything.
>
> Best,
>
> Homeowner

Crafting an Effective SDS

If, for some reason, you can't complete the SDS immediately after the conversation or meeting, I suggest you take real-time notes.

They can simply be word prompts of what you'll subsequently put in the SDS.

A good SDS lists the key takeaways, which typically include: (a) commitments made—who will do what by when, (b) critical facts or understandings where divergent memories or interpretations could be problematic, and (c) recognition of positive or constructive behavior. Chances are, you'll be thinking about expected future action, whatever it might be:

- "I agreed to do the following by the following date."
- "You agreed to do the following by the following date."
- "Our plan going forward is X."
- "We've agreed on the following."
- "Here's what's going to happen next."

The most effective SDSs tend to be the shortest. A few bullet points, and that's it. To keep it short, ask yourself, "Is anything said in this conversation or meeting worth preserving in writing?" If your answer is yes, craft a succinct SDS. And because it is succinct, an SDS promotes constructive go-forward exchanges: What can we agree on? Where do we go from here? Who's going to do what by when?

In my experience, the benefits of an SDS extend beyond the document itself. They include the focus and discipline you must develop to write an effective SDS after the meeting or discussion. They help keep the focus on facts not feelings. Think about how many time-wasting meetings you've attended and unproductive conversations you've had. Would that meeting or conversation have benefited from the focus and discipline provided when the parties know that a short, targeted summary will follow?

BENEFITS OF THE SDS FORMAT

- Because they're written while the conversation is fresh in mind, they're usually accurate.

- Because they are limited to summarizing only the key takeaways, SDSs take minutes to write.

- When sent promptly with language such as "Let me know if I missed or misstated anything," they're user-friendly for recipients. Recipients don't need to reply unless they think the writer missed something significant.

- In a non-judgmental, non-authoritarian way, the SDS aligns the writer and recipient. It provides a checklist they can use to hold themselves and each other accountable.

Email is a handy SDS vehicle. In addition to being quick and efficient, email makes it easy to store SDSs electronically. After hitting "Send," click and drag the SDS into a labeled folder. This makes subsequent retrieval quick and easy.

Don't Make These SDS Mistakes

Are there missteps to avoid? Yes. Here are the three most common:

1. *Wordiness.* You're not taking meeting minutes, and you

don't get points for comprehensiveness. List only the most important items addressed, such as specific commitments or deadlines. If the recipient thinks you missed something, they can respond to your invitation to make corrections. Less is more.

2. *Continuing the conversation.* Don't add, embellish, reflect, opine, etc. The conversation is over. You're simply memorializing its critical points. The SDS is a summary of a real-time conversation, not a substitute.

3. *Delay.* Research shows that we start to forget new information almost as quickly as we learn it. The longer you wait, the greater the likelihood that your SDS will omit or misstate something important. Also, delaying makes it harder to write the SDS because you'll have to rack your memory regarding what was said. Memory study pioneer Hermann Ebbinghaus essentially found that our brains are sieves. We start forgetting things within hours, if not minutes. He called it the "forgetting curve."

THE SDS AS THE HR CULTURE COACH'S GO-TO TOOL

The CHRO at a large international manufacturing company once said to me, "Jathan, I've learned a lot from you. However, nothing compares to the value of the Same Day Summary. In fact, whenever we hire a new member of the HR team, I personally teach them the technique and make it clear they'd better commit it to practice."

THE HR CULTURE COACH AS ORGANIZATION SDS GURU

In addition to applying the SDS as a tool, I strongly recommend that HR teach, coach, and support management in its use of the SDS. The SDS's benefits are by no means limited to HR. Spreading the use of SDSs will be another major HR organization value-add.

As I mention with the listening techniques in the previous chapter, although the SDS is simple, simple doesn't mean easy—at least at first. When I coach others on its use, I typically find that it takes a few practice sessions before my coachee has mastered it.

I suggest you, as HR Culture Coach, do what I do as SDS coach. If you can turn things around quickly, have the coachee email you a draft of the SDS they intend to send. Otherwise, review the coachee's SDSs for potential improvement. A few practice sessions and they won't need you anymore.

What are the uses? In the HR world, this includes but is not limited to performance management (discussed in the next chapter), discipline & discharge (discussed in Chapter 6), health-related employee accommodations, investigations, follow-up messages to meetings held, delegating responsibility, go-forward conflict resolution agreements, interactions with vendors, and sessions when HR coaches or advises management or others.

In fact, there really are no limitations to the SDS's use. Put simply: Any real-time conversation you think has significance merits an SDS.

ENABLING EFFECTIVE DELEGATION WITH PERGIVENESS

Alongside encouraging widespread use of the SDS as a more frequent form of communication (and reducing the need for documentation), my other favorite communication tool is what I call a "pergiveness" memo or message. It's a mix of asking for "permission" and begging for "forgiveness." I use pergiveness memos both to communicate with my bosses and as a required form of communication from my direct reports. Pergiveness messages come in handy when a real-time conversation is not feasible, yet the matter is of some urgency.

The pergiveness tool grew out of my frustration as a middle manager. At the time, I managed the Portland and Seattle offices of a large international law firm. My boss, Chuck, worked out of the Indianapolis office and had a bunch of other offices to oversee in addition to tending his full book of legal business.

I repeatedly found myself trapped in indecision. I'd email Chuck proposing to do something and asking for his okay. Sometimes, it came with a yes, or sometimes with a no, but more often than not, time went by without a response. I'd end up having to send a follow-up and sometimes even a follow-up to a follow-up.

So instead of asking for Chuck's okay or even his view, I started sending him "pergiveness" messages. It worked so well that I taught the technique to the office administrator who reported to me and told her to use it on me!

Here's how pergiveness works: Before you act, you send a message saying:

- What you're going to do.

- Why you're doing it.

- When you'll do it.

- A statement like, "Let me know if you have any questions or wish to discuss this."

If you don't hear from the person(s) by the date or time you stated, go for it! Why is this tool so effective?

- If I'm your boss, pergiveness gives you the freedom to act, and it gives me the freedom *not* to act. I can tell you to wait, that we need to talk first. Or I can say "Great!" Or I can do . . . nothing.

- Pergiveness promotes effective delegation and keeps business moving forward. A leader and their reports can discuss which things fall into what category: permission, forgiveness, or pergiveness. This approach creates a healthy balance between micromanagement and rogue subordinate action. This way, leaders don't worry about what their team is doing and don't need to control everything.

UPSKILLING COMMUNICATION

Let me reiterate that I'm not saying documentation is evil. It has its place in the function of HR as in all other departments. Instead, what I'm encouraging is that as you embrace a Culture Coach role, you think more about what types of communication will help the organization work more effectively and less about documenting each potential infraction of complex rules. Above all:

- Favor real-time communication whenever possible. Talk to people!

- For any conversation you think is important to follow up on, send a Same Day Summary (SDS).

- Use pergiveness memos or messages to enable delegation and more rapid action.

CHAPTER 5

A Performance Management System That Works Better for Employers than Lawyers

M y first boss was arguably my best one.

In high school, I had a part-time job moving furniture at a weekend auction. My job was straightforward—unload the trucks, position the furniture properly to be auctioned, and, when I heard the word "Sold!" quickly move the furniture off the stage and replace it with the next item to be auctioned. Then, after the customers went home, I'd reload the trucks.

Hard work, but for a high school student in rural Indiana in the early 1970s, ten bucks an hour was a fortune! And in cash!

My boss went by "Buddy." Short of height, barrel-chested, bald head, thick arms, supersize belly, and an Irish accent, Buddy made it crystal clear what he expected: move furniture quickly, safely, and in its proper order.

Buddy's feedback was continual. Both kinds. On one occasion, after a huge amount of furniture had been sold, Buddy punched me in the arm—ouch!—took a ten-spot out of his wallet and handed it to me. "You worked your ass off. This is some extra from me to you." (The extra cash was welcome, but the punch I could've done without.)

On the other hand, there were times when I got feedback of a different sort. "Janove! What the hell is the matter with you?! Bend with your %*&@!$*@ knees!"

Since Buddy, I've had a great many bosses, mostly more sophisticated, educated, experienced, etc. Yet none of them did as good a job as Buddy in letting me know what was expected of me and how I was doing in meeting those expectations.

And isn't meeting (or exceeding) expectations what performance reviews are all about? Yet, as I discuss next, most performance review systems would themselves receive a failing grade. If you want a system that provides employees with timely information to help them actually improve, you need to rethink annual performance reviews from the viewpoint of a Culture Coach instead of a Compliance Cop. In this chapter, I talk about all the problems with performance reviews (most of which you've probably experienced yourself) and talk about a system for replacing them with more frequent reviews that provide meaningful information, improving accountability and employee performance.

THE BAD PERFORMANCE OF REVIEWS

I've spoken at numerous HR conferences. Sometimes, I begin with, "Please raise your hand if your organization uses some form of performance review."

Invariably, a sea of hands rises. I then ask: "Do you agree with the following statement? 'The performance review is well worth the time and effort it takes based on its return in employee performance, accountability, and engagement.'"

Instantly, the sea of hands dissolves.

In the Introduction of this book, I share study results concerning when performance reviews showed up in employment litigation. The study demonstrated that at least one group benefits from performance reviews: plaintiffs' lawyers!

For all other groups, the picture isn't so rosy. For example, a Gallup survey reported that 95 percent of managers say their organization's performance review system doesn't work, and a mere *2 percent* of chief human resource officers believe their company's performance management works.[1]

Why such dismal results? Several reasons:

1. When it comes to relationships with others, human beings aren't rational, analytical creatures. Not even engineers! Conventional performance reviews endeavor to make rational what can't be made rational. With the advent of

Artificial Intelligence (AI), I fear this problem will only get worse. See Chapter 2 for more discussion about using AI effectively.

2. Typical performance review forms are very user-*un*friendly. Instead of managers viewing them as opportunities to improve workplace relationships, they consider them a big pain in the you-know-what. This attitude contributes to HR playing Compliance Cop, as it chases down and harangues dilatory managers.

3. Performance reviews substitute delayed written communication for real-time oral communication. As I explain in Chapter 4, when the topic is in any way sensitive, communicating first in writing is almost always a big mistake. Moreover, delayed feedback is always a bad idea. It invariably makes things worse.

4. Performance reviews often are tied to money, such as bonuses or pay raises. In my experience, this approach skews the process in a very unhealthy direction. I'm not a robotic paycheck casher. I'm a human being! "One of the first things I did at Netflix," notes Patty McCord in her book, *Powerful: Building a Culture of Freedom and Responsibility*, "was to decouple our pay system from the feedback process."[2]

5. Most performance review forms don't zero in on what truly matters—the most important things the manager believes the employee needs to do to be successful in their position.

To replace this faulty system, I've developed an alternative performance management system that I've taught, coached, and practiced. When supported by executive leadership and proactively implemented by HR, it truly works. Three necessary tools comprise my recommended performance management system:

1. The active listening techniques I describe in Chapter 2

2. The Same Day Summary (SDS) I describe in the previous chapter

3. The Star Profile (SP), which I describe in this chapter

Let me first describe the Star Profile. Then, I'll show how these components come together to create a performance management system that actually helps improve performance.

THE STAR PROFILE

In a small handful of sentences and words, an SP captures the most needed behaviors or actions in a particular job from the perspective of key stakeholders, primarily including the employee's boss. It's not a traditional job description, and it's not a statement of qualifications, conditions, or competencies. It's a mini-movie script of action that will lead the moviegoer to say, "Yes! I really like this picture!"

Perhaps ironically, the SP concept originated during my employment litigation career. When defending wrongful discharge claims, I found that when I crafted a good story, it was a lot more effective with investigators, arbitrators, judges, or juries. Instead of the conventional, "Your Honor, the plaintiff's race discrimination and retaliation claim fails for the following seventeen reasons," I told a story of why termination was the right thing to do.

To do this, I had to get my clients out of defensive mode—"We didn't do anything wrong! He was a bad employee!"

I'd say, "Before telling me what was wrong with this employee, I'd like to know more about the job. What actions or behaviors are needed for a person in this position to be successful in terms of performance, reliability, and interactions with others? What really matters and why?"

Once the client fleshed this out for me, I shifted to, "Okay, now tell me where and how this employee fell short. Describe the impact and why it mattered." I then crafted a defense based on what they shared.

That description of what is needed to succeed in a job is what I now call a *Star Profile*. I haven't litigated a case in fifteen years. Yet the Star Profile has become a core element of the work I currently do as an organization consultant and executive coach.

Essentially, Star Profiles aren't performance-centric so much as they are relationship-centric. Employee performance isn't the end; it's a means to a mutually satisfying and successful long-term relationship. In my experience, if you get the relationship right, desired performance almost always follows.

When I coach leaders on creating SPs for their reports, we start with a generic model. It covers the three categories that most likely distinguish success from failure.

- **Productivity**: Produces high-quality and quantity work that is aligned with the most desired results.

- **Reliability**: Can be counted on to be where and when needed; reachable and responsive.

- **Culture**: Supports a culture grounded in trust, respect, civility, and collaboration.

We then customize the generic model for the specific position, zeroing in on what matters most. A good example is the SP Rob Moore created and used with Louonna Kachur, as I recount in Chapter 1. Here's another example.

Star Profile for an Office Administrator

When I became the office managing shareholder in a large international law firm, I replaced someone with a very different management style. My predecessor pretty much did all of the thinking and oversaw all of the details. The office administrator (OA) simply followed orders.

I desired something close to the opposite: an OA to whom I could delegate office management responsibilities early, often, and to the greatest degree possible. This meant a huge change for the incumbent OA.

I crafted the following Star Profile:

- Leads and models professional, productive, and team-oriented office behavior.

- Anticipates, troubleshoots, follows up, and follows through with office, staff, attorneys, and home office needs.

- Loops me in efficiently.

USING A STAR PROFILE TO IMPROVE PERFORMANCE

Now that you know what a Star Profile is, here's how to put it to good use.

- Step 1: Craft a Star Profile for each position reporting to you. Have a real-time, interactive conversation with each employee about what you wrote and why. Follow up with an SDS. When review time comes, the SP will anchor the discussion.

- Step 2: In the performance review discussion, use the No-FEAR listening technique. The "F" in this technique is a candid, succinct summation of how the employee has done with respect to each prong of the SP. Then, switch to active listening (EAR). Use this discussion as an opportunity to celebrate successes and accomplishments, as well as to constructively address needed change.

- Step 3: The last step is the SDS that you'll write and give to the employee *after* the meeting. It captures what you consider to be the key takeaways from the discussion you just had.

TIP: REPLACE ANNUAL REVIEWS WITH QUARTERLY CONVERSATIONS

I recommend using your SPs quarterly as the basis of productive conversations around topics like what's working, what could be improved, and what the goals should be. (Along with what, if anything, needs to change in the SP itself.)

To continue the OA example I started previously, here's how I used it with the administrator.

As I explained to her, each sentence reflected the behaviors or actions I most desired. I needed someone who would promote a healthy office culture; proactively prevent and solve problems arising with the office, staff, attorneys, and our home office; and figure out when and how I needed to be informed *and* when I didn't.

Our discussion of these three sentences went beyond the "what" of the job to the "why" and to my OA taking ownership of the "how." Through our discussion of the SP, she had a clear picture of the big picture—the vision and goals underlying each SP sentence—and how she could play a pivotal role in my success as managing shareholder.

After that initial conversation, I met with her quarterly to discuss her performance against the three clearly defined criteria. Each time, I consciously used the techniques described in Chapter 2, meaning our performance review sessions were led by listening instead of telling. It was a two-way street. We both gained from the discussion.

I then followed up each conversation with a Same Day Summary that captured the key points and anchored us until the next review session. Here's an example.

To: _____

From: Jathan

Today's date: _____

Re: Summary of Q3 2024 performance discussion

Dear _____,

Here's a summary of key takeaways from our discussion this morning. Please let me know if I missed anything.

Regarding the first sentence of your SP, I've been very impressed with your leadership. Thank you!

Regarding the second sentence, again you've been very proactive in anticipating needs and issues and in acting quickly to solve problems that arise. Thank you!

As for the third sentence, we agreed that this is an area of needed improvement. Instead of running every decision by me, you'll first determine which category the decision falls into: (1) "Permission," meaning you don't act without my prior approval; (2) "Forgiveness," meaning you act without advance notice to me; or (3) "Pergiveness," meaning you send me an email stating what you intend to do, when, and why. If I don't respond by the time you specify, you act.

Looking forward to next quarter!

Best,

Jathan

Another SP Example: HR Business Partner

Let's assume I'm an HR director whose direct reports include HR business partners (BPs) who work directly with company managers and employees. Here's what my SP would look like:

- Maintains a working understanding of applicable HR-related laws and regulations.
- Works with our managers and employees as a coach, not a cop.
- Collaboratively supports fellow members of our HR team.

THE 3-3-1 TECHNIQUE

My favorite 360° assessment tool is derived from the work of Marshall Goldsmith. I call it the "3-3-1." For each employee whose performance I am reviewing, I confidentially ask others the following:

- What are the person's greatest strengths (up to *three*)?
- What are areas where growth or improvement would be beneficial (up to *three*)?
- If you identify more than one growth area, which *one* should we focus on first and what practical improvement suggestions do you have?

Prior to the performance review, I would meet with each of my BPs to discuss the SP and ensure a shared understanding of what each bullet really means: What "working understanding" means. What the coach vs. cop difference is. What "collaboratively" means.

Each meeting would be followed with an SDS. When review time comes, I would do a 360° assessment in which I confidentially ask a representative sample of managers, employees, and other members of the HR department how the BP has done regarding the SP and what improvement suggestions they may have.

Next, I would meet with each of my BPs and review how they've done using the No-FEAR method. Lastly, I'd write an SDS and preserve it for future review and discussion. Here's an example:

To: BP Sarah

From: Jathan

Today's date: _____

Re: Summary of Q4 2024 performance discussion

Hi Sarah,

Here's a summary of key takeaways from our conversation this morning. Please let me know if I missed anything.

Regarding the first sentence of your SP, you have maintained a solid understanding of applicable law. To keep yourself up to date, you plan to attend the online program "Employment Law for HR Professionals." I expressed my encouragement that you continue to seek out these types of opportunities.

Regarding the second sentence, we discussed that although your goal is to be seen as a coach, you are sometimes perceived as more of a "cop." You and I agreed to spend more time together doing role-plays on effectively combining compliance with coaching in your interactions with managers and employees. Also, we agreed to connect you to some outside coaching and training on executive coaching concepts and techniques.

As for the third sentence, everyone considers you to be a great team player who is always willing to lend a hand. As I said, I personally appreciate and am grateful for the wonderful service you provide!

Best,

Jathan

TIPS FOR EFFECTIVE USE OF SPS AS PERFORMANCE MANAGEMENT TOOLS

As I just mentioned, because this process is efficient and user-friendly, it lends itself to being done more often than annually. I recommend quarterly. Here are some other tips:

- *Constructive candor.* The focus should be on progress and solutions, not finger-pointing. Wherever possible, follow Stakeholder Centered Coaching cofounder Marshall Goldsmith's advice: Replace feedback with feedforward. Instead of the rearview mirror (what happened), keep your primary attention on the road ahead (what will make the journey safe and successful for all).

- *No surprises.* The performance review should be a summary, *not* a substitute for real-time feedback and feedforward.

- *No money.* Don't obscure what really matters with money. The focus should remain on the needs, priorities, and goals of the job and your relationship with your employees. The message should be, "Technically speaking, I'm your boss. Yet, in reality, I'm your partner as we work together to make this organization a better place."

LIMITATIONS OF CONTINGENT REWARDS

Another aspect of NOT bringing money into the SP-based performance conversation is clearly stated by *NYT* best-selling author Daniel Pink. In an email to me in 2024, he discussed what he calls "controlling contingent rewards," which are framed as "if/then" statements (*If you do this, then you get that*). Such statements are mainstays of company compensation systems. He wrote, "Most research shows that these types of rewards boost performance for simple tasks with short time horizons. But they're far less effective—at times even counterproductive—for complex tasks with long time horizons."[3]

- *No scorecards.* The performance review should be relationship-centric not performance-centric. If you and I are in a reporting relationship and it's healthy, vibrant, and vigorous, we will have more than enough opportunities to identify and pursue shared goals. On the other hand, if our relationship isn't healthy, a goal-oriented performance review isn't going to fix things; more likely it will make both of us more frustrated.

The SP process I've outlined works for all positions, including hourly. Although my first boss, Buddy, didn't call what he did a Star Profile, he used the process. His SP was a single sentence: "Moves furniture quickly, safely and in proper order." For another example of an SP for an hourly employee, here's what a client restaurant group crafted and used.

STAR BUSSER

1. At the ready to expedite the efficient turning of the dining room.

2. Owns responsibility for the professional appearance of themselves and their entire restaurant.

IMPLEMENTING A STAR PROFILE-BASED SYSTEM

For this SP-based performance review process to work in organizations with many employees, HR support is indispensable. Here are my suggested steps that HR leaders can take:

· **Step 1:** Learn, apply, and model the SP performance review process within the HR department. To paraphrase Mahatma Gandhi, HR must be the change it wishes to see.

- **Step 2:** Create a document retention system preserving the SPs and SDSs.

- **Step 3:** Continually train and coach your managers. SPs and SDSs are simple. That doesn't mean they're easy—at least at first. Until they get the process down, which may take more than one quarterly review cycle, your managers will need proactive HR support.

- **Step 4:** Follow up and assess progress. This includes troubleshooting any problems that arise. It also includes sharing success stories where the process dramatically improved a manager–employee relationship, as attested to by both parties. In my experience, sharing success stories can provide the proverbial tipping point—the early followers generate momentum for the rest to follow.

REPLACING ANNUAL REVIEWS WITH QUARTERLY CONVERSATIONS

As an employee yourself, think about what kinds of systems would help you actually get better at your job. It isn't a once-a-year formal conversation. You need feedback more regularly and a conversation based on how you're performing relative to what truly matters.

Creating that new system is the job of a Culture Coach. Approaching performance management this way will help create a work culture where employees understand what is expected of them and know specifically what they need to do to improve. Hasn't that been the goal all along?

CHAPTER 6

It's Time to Fire "Progressive" Discipline

This chapter makes the case that there's a much better way to deal with employee disciplinary problems than conventional progressive discipline, where penalties for failure to achieve goals or reforms get increasingly harsh. As a former employment law attorney and now executive coach, I've never experienced anything "progressive" about that conventional approach to discipline. In my view, it's a pernicious contradiction in terms. It's negative, adversarial, blame-oriented, punishment-oriented, and usually accompanied by a threat ending with "will subject you to further disciplinary action, up to and including discharge." Ugh!

Conventional forms of discipline are also usually documentation-oriented—another problem—replacing real-time, human-to-human exchanges. (A mistake I discuss in Chapter 8 is that "Read and sign this document" is not a dialogue. And as I explain in Chapter 4, research has shown that we react more negatively to written words than to spoken ones.)

Further, an adversarial disciplinary system often leads to demeaning treatment when an employee is discharged: They are marched out of the workplace without a shred of dignity. As I explain in Chapter 9, adding insult to injury often prompts a desire for revenge via the legal system. A prominent California plaintiffs' attorney once told me, "My work would be cut in half if employers were kinder and smarter about how they let employees go."

In my experience, too many PIP (performance improvement plan) systems suffer the same drawbacks as disciplinary systems, especially those that have grown out of a Compliance Cop mentality. They usually fail to achieve their stated purpose, "performance improvement," and the returns are usually dismal. PIPs more often embitter the employee than motivate them to improve. There might be temporary improvement, but it won't be sustained, resulting in a vicious "PIP cycle."

So instead of firing the employee through conventional means, Culture Coaches are more likely to fire the PIP, the disciplinary demotion, the "First Warning; Second Warning; Final Warning," "Verbal Counseling," "Corrective Action," "Last Chance Agreement," and similar nonsense.

"Now what?" you may ask. Here's the Culture Coach answer.

DISCIPLINE & DISCHARGE BASED ON FIT NOT FEAR

When it comes to employee discipline and discharge, the Culture Coach approach is based on respect. We don't judge people. We don't punish people. We don't try to frighten employees into compliance. Instead, we hold conversations with employees about expectations and commitments, clearly state consequences, and aim for a better fit between employees and jobs.

When problems arise, such as an employee falling short of our expectations, our approach is to explore with the employee whether there is some intervention by which the employee can correct the problem and meet our expectations thereafter. If we determine that there isn't an intervention we are reasonably confident might correct the problem and that the employee needs to leave the company, we continue to adhere to the principle of respect. It's not that the departing employee is a bad person. It's that the fit is not right between that person and what we need in that position.

By no means am I suggesting that problematic employee behavior should be overlooked. Quite the contrary. It's how you address the problem that makes the difference. Next are four rules followed by Culture Coaches. After briefly describing each rule, I give some examples that show how they work in real life.

Rule #1: Avoid Avoidance

Homo sapiens comes naturally with what I call the "instinct to avoid." Mother Nature imbues us with a hair-trigger threat detector. Out for a walk in the woods? "Hmmm, is that a stick or is it a snake?" Actually, you won't be calmly and rationally analyzing this question. Instead, your threat-recognition system shuts off your reasoning brain. Your body assumes it's a snake until proven otherwise and responds by leaving the scene as quickly as possible. Threat avoided.

Over the millennia, this instinct has, no doubt, served our species well. However, I don't think it helps us in today's workplace. Just the opposite, in fact.

When something goes wrong at work and it's our job to address it, there's an immediate fear of confronting the person we think is responsible for it. Instead of promptly, directly, and specifically confronting the employee, we worry, "How might he react?" "She could get mad." "He might retaliate." Or Heaven forbid! "She may go to HR!" Negative speculation replaces needed action.

Inevitably, instead of solving the workplace problem, the avoidance instinct makes it worse. The problem festers and grows until it becomes unmanageable and finally *has* to be dealt with—only, by now, the opportunity for a constructive resolution is gone. When the person releases their pent-up frustrations—"I can't take it anymore!"—it takes the employee by surprise. The exchange is almost always hostile. In the employee's mind, insult has been added to injury.

In my view, managers and employees need to learn how to ski (metaphorically speaking). After I moved from the Midwest to Salt Lake City, I decided to learn how to ski. Like almost all beginning skiers, I had to overcome a natural, seemingly self-protective instinct. When about to ski down a hill, I'd look at the downhill slope and fear going too fast, being out of control, and ending up in a heap of ski equipment and body parts. A little voice would whisper in my ear, "Downhill momentum is the danger, so counterbalance it by leaning back toward the uphill slope."

My ski instructor urged me to do the opposite—put weight forward on my skis toward the downhill slope. That seemed completely counterintuitive. *Is she trying to get me killed?* I thought. Yet every time that I ignored her advice and trusted my instinct, what happened? I went too fast, got out of control, and ended up in a heap.

To ski safely and effectively, I had to overcome this natural threat-recognition instinct. Instead, I conditioned it to serve as a behavioral trigger to do the opposite.

There's a close parallel between skiing and dealing with workplace problems. The instinct to avoid confrontation is just like the beginning skier's instinct to lean away from the downhill slope. Both arise from the mistaken notion that avoidance means safety. Yet, in both cases, the opposite is true.

Just like skiers, managers and employees need to be coached on converting their avoidance instinct into a trigger to do the opposite, even when it seems counterintuitive. Instead of putting the employee problem at the bottom of or even off the agenda, put it at the very top. Weight forward on skis means heading directly toward what causes you anxiety. Confront the problem without delay. Do it directly, preferably face-to-face and in real time. Discuss the facts with the employee and do it with a solution-oriented mindset—"How do we fix this problem?"—as opposed to "Who's to blame?"

Rule #2: Have No-FEAR Confrontations

As I describe in Chapter 2, this technique has four components. The first is *Frame*—you briefly and directly state the problem; no beating around the bush. Next, you go into active listening mode using your "EAR"—*Explore* the other person's view, ask them to *Acknowledge* that you understand them, and then and only then *Respond* with your point of view.

Rule #3: Don't Use Prebaked Disciplinary Documents

Replace standard disciplinary documents with the Same Day Summary. As I describe in Chapter 4, the SDS briefly summarizes what the writer believes are the key takeaways from a meeting or discussion just held.

Although the SDS lacks the traditional bells and whistles of a written warning and doesn't require the employee's signature, an SDS actually decreases claim risk. Why? Because employees are more likely to feel they were treated fairly and with respect. The relationship is less likely to become hostile, even if it ends. Anger doesn't rise to the level that it motivates an employee to seek an attorney.

Rule #4: Have Crossroads Conversations

The Crossroads Conversation is a variation of the No-FEAR technique. You begin by *framing* the conversation with a statement that the status quo is no longer acceptable. Only two roads are left.

Either the employee makes the necessary changes, or they leave the organization. No third option.

Then, after the *frame*, pivot into active EAR listening mode.

DEMOTE DEMOTIONS

I've encountered many situations where, instead of a problem employee being let go, they are demoted. This approach invariably proves to be a mistake, which is why I advocate the Crossroads Conversation (improve or leave). "Love the people who work for you," Marshall Goldsmith told me. "If not, let them go. Don't kick them and expect them to be grateful."[1]

The one exception is if the employee genuinely wants the job, and the employer genuinely believes the employee will be a good fit for the role. An example might be a successful salesperson who was promoted to sales manager but struggled in that position. If the person genuinely wants to return to their former role, then the demotion (it's really a reassignment) could work. However, the presumption should still be separation from employment.

THE RULES IN ACTION

Here are two examples that show how the four rules of discipline come together to help resolve performance issues.

Example One: Tardiness Problem

Let's say you are my boss. My shift begins at 8 a.m. You observe that I arrive at 8:10. You say to me, "Jathan, it's eight-ten, and your shift begins at eight. What happened?"

Your first sentence succinctly *frames* the conversation. You don't blame. You don't threaten. You don't go into detail. You simply state the issue and then immediately shift into active listening EAR mode. Your "E" (Explore) question doesn't contain any judgment or opinion. There are no assumptions. You don't ask, "Why are you late?" Your question is purely curiosity-based, seeking information.

If this is my first time being late, and assuming I make a commitment to be on time henceforth, you may or may not follow up with an SDS.

If the problem continues, however, it's definitely time to use the SDS. "Jathan, I'm concerned. Last week, you came in at eight-ten on Wednesday and said you'd take the necessary steps to prevent this problem from occurring again. Yet today, you came in at eight-twenty. What happened?" Again, the issue is framed without judgment and the question seeks information.

Assuming you now have my attention and I make an unequivocal commitment to be on time, you say, "Good. I need that commitment. To keep us on the same page, I will be sending you a brief summary of this conversation. Let me know if I miss anything."

To: Jathan

From: You

Date: Today

Re: Summary of today's discussion

Jathan, here's a summary of our conversation. Please let me know if I missed anything.

- I pointed out that you arrived today at 8:20 a.m. and that last Wednesday, you arrived at 8:10 a.m., which we discussed at that time.

- I emphasized that it's necessary that you be here reliably at 8 a.m.

- You apologized and gave me your assurance you will do what's necessary so that I can rely on you being here at your scheduled time.

Best,

You

What if I come in late yet again or respond to your question by pushing back with "I don't know, boss, that I can consistently be on time, and I don't think being late now and then is such a big deal"? I'm essentially guaranteeing repeat problematic behavior. It's time for the Crossroads Conversation.

"Jathan, if that's the case, I don't see how you can remain at our company since I have to be able to rely on you being here every workday at eight. It may be time to end your employment here. What do you think?"

In my experience, the most common responses are either: (a) I change my position and describe to you the steps I will take to ensure being on time (in which case you send me another SDS) or (b) I leave the company quietly and without fuss (in which case you do an SDS to file).

Essentially, you're maximizing the likelihood that I make the necessary change, or you're ensuring that my departure will be handled with civility and respect. It's not that I'm a bad employee or a bad person. It's simply that I don't fit the requirements of the job. It may also be important to note that I was given the opportunity to meet the requirements, but for whatever reason, I chose not to.

Example Two: Problematic Associate Attorney Behavior

As I mentioned, in my prior career, I managed the Portland and Seattle offices of a large international law firm. I received reports that one of our associate attorneys, "Sam," was behaving badly. Partners complained that Sam was unreliable, hard to get ahold of, turned work in at the last minute, and sometimes missed deadlines altogether. In addition, staff members complained that he often became angry, demeaning, and intimidating, especially when under pressure due to impending deadlines.

I scheduled a meeting with Sam, employed the No-FEAR and Crossroads techniques, and then followed up with an SDS.

To: Sam

From: Jathan

Date: Today

Re: Our meeting this morning

Sam, here's a summary of key takeaways from today's meeting. Please let me know if you think I missed or misstated anything.

We discussed the complaints from partners about your turning work in late and being hard to contact. We also discussed complaints from staff, who felt you can be intimidating and disrespectful, especially when there's a last-minute rush to meet deadlines.

I shared with you that as managing partner, I consider three characteristics to be essential for an associate attorney to remain employed here and hopefully to eventually make partner:

- Produces first-rate, efficient work.

- Zealously responsive to internal and external client needs.

- Treats everyone at all times with civility and respect.

As I mentioned, the partners consider you a talented attorney clearly capable of first-rate work. As I also explained, it's the other two characteristics that are problematic. The partners are the "internal clients" primarily responsible for the firm's relationship with the external clients who pay our bills. And, regardless of their position or pay level, *everyone* in this firm is entitled to respect and civility at all times.

I appreciate your response that, although you were surprised no one had said anything to you directly, you will concentrate on getting assignments done earlier, make sure people can contact you when needed, and, even when under stress, not take it out on staff.

Thank you for making this commitment. As I said, I hope that you make major strides in those two areas so that your relationship with this firm continues.

Over the next thirty days, I will be checking in with partners and staff and will let you know what progress has been made.

If you have questions or would like to discuss this further, please let me know.

Best,

Jathan

This was the approach I took with most problems. In this particular case, "Sam" ended up leaving the firm amicably. However, in most of the others, the desired change occurred and was sustained. Regardless of outcome, this approach always worked. In most cases, the employee made the necessary changes. In the other cases, they left the firm without acrimony or fuss.

RESPECT-BASED DISCIPLINE

Aside from my role as manager, in different capacities, I've worked with numerous managers, executives, and other organization leaders. Based on these many experiences, I can say that when it comes to employee discipline and discharge, please, please don't assume conventional wisdom is wise!

As you can see by the examples I've given in this chapter, Culture Coaches do not ignore discipline, performance, or behavior problems. They do the exact opposite. They act more quickly than is typical in a Compliance Cop environment. And, equally important, everything they do is based on respect for both the employee *and* business needs. They talk with the employee immediately (or as soon as practical), use active questioning and listening to elicit information from the employee, clearly spell out expectations in the conversation (confirmed by an SDS), then act accordingly depending on whether the problem disappears or reappears.

CHAPTER 7

Improve Hiring and Promotion by Avoiding the "Stupid Switch"

Personal confession: To my everlasting chagrin, my Stupid Switch has been flipped on both as an employer doing the hiring and as a job applicant naively thinking I'd finally found the promised land.

What do I mean by the "Stupid Switch"? It refers to common mistakes people make during a hiring or promotion process because of untested assumptions. Here are its manifestations:

1. Ability to *get* the job conflated with ability to *do* the job.

2. Ability to do current job conflated with ability to do job employee is promoted or transferred to.

3. State of recruitment conflated with actual life on the job.

The Stupid Switch applies to both employer and applicant/employee. At the heart of the problem is how both sides view the hiring process. Instead of a mutual exploration to determine the likelihood of a long-term fit, they approach it as a contest. The applicant "scores" when she gets an offer. The employer "scores" when it gets acceptance of the offer it makes. This game makes the parties vulnerable to overselling and underevaluating.

In Chapter 5, I introduce a tool favored by Culture Coaches called the Star Profile, which is a few sentences and keywords that capture the most needed behaviors or actions necessary for a person to succeed in a particular job. It is a multipurpose tool, perhaps the most important of which is its role in hiring and promotion decisions. For example, in Chapter 1, I share the story of Louonna Kachur and Rob Moore, in which a Star Profile played a key role in an employee selection decision and in Louonna's retention and ultimate professional success.

In this chapter, I share two additional Star Profile stories that demonstrate its effectiveness in hiring and promotion situations. One story addresses how to use the Star Profile to avoid making a bad hiring decision, and the other addresses how to use the Star Profile to avoid making a bad promotion/successorship decision. In addition, I'll show how to use Star Profiles as both due diligence and recruitment devices and explore the vital role HR can play in improving the odds from coin toss to assured long-term success.

GOOD AT *GETTING* A JOB VS. *DOING* IT

"Rebecca" was the director of a fairly new Jewish Studies Department at a university. The university had been able to afford only one full-time, tenure-track position—hers.

Things changed after a wealthy donor agreed to endow another position. This meant she would finally have a colleague, her very own associate director.

With eagerness, Rebecca jumped into the university process for hiring a professor. She formed a search committee and began looking for a fellow scholar to join her.

During the search process, Rebecca and I had a conversation about Star Profiles and how they're used to make hiring decisions.

Several months later, Rebecca called me to say that the search committee had narrowed the finalists to five and was about to fly the first one in for interviews, faculty meetings, and a guest lecture.

Based on Rebecca's expressed desires and needs, we came up with the following Star Profile:

ASSOCIATE DIRECTOR, JEWISH STUDIES

1. Provides teaching that attracts students to our program.

2. Produces tenure-worthy scholarship.

3. Interacts with members of the community to promote interest in and support for our program.

4. Collaborates with and supports the Director in furthering the program's goals.

Rebecca explained to me the "why" behind her four sentences.

The first characteristic of attracting students is because "we are a relatively new program. It will be critical to have the kind of teacher who makes students want to attend our courses and get the word out to other students."

The second characteristic was important to Rebecca because she wasn't looking for an academic superstar. "Such a person," she said, "will probably spend too much time on research and want to leave once he or she gets an offer from a more prestigious university." Rebecca noted that, on the other hand, "This person must produce academic work of sufficient quality to get tenure. Otherwise, I'll have a problem in the future. I need a good balance."

The third characteristic, promoting interest and support, was key because Rebecca's program didn't have much money. "We depend on outside support. I need an associate director who interacts well with people who aren't fellow scholars yet can help us."

Rebecca explained the fourth and final characteristic of collaboration this way: "I'm going to have to work with this person extremely closely. Trust is an absolute. I need a colleague with whom I can truly collaborate."

The first finalist to arrive was Joseph, a candidate who had already established a reputation as an up-and-coming scholar. His curriculum vitae was probably the most impressive of the five finalists.

Joseph's guest lecture was a smashing success. It dripped with brilliance and authoritative elocution.

That evening, Rebecca hosted a reception for Joseph at her home. Fellow faculty members, as well as program donors and community supporters, wandered through her kitchen, dining area, and living room with drinks and food. I was one of them.

After a while, I noticed that Joseph had been locked in a circle with three professors in an animated discussion. They seemed oblivious to everyone else. I pulled Rebecca aside and suggested she test the Star Profile. I said, "From what you've told me, Joseph won't have a problem with profile characteristics one and two, the ability to teach effectively and produce tenure-worthy scholarship. But," I added, "I'm not so sure about characteristic three, interacting with members of the community to support the program."

Rebecca decided to try a test. She tapped Joseph on the shoulder and said, "Excuse me, Joseph, may I speak with you for a moment?"

Joseph stepped out of the circle and faced her. "If you don't mind," she said, "before people start leaving, I'd like to introduce you. And if you'd care to say a few words, that would be great."

"I have not prepared remarks for this occasion," Joseph said.

"That's fine," Rebecca said. "You don't have to say anything substantial, just maybe a greeting and an impromptu word or two."

With a serious tone, Joseph said, "I don't do impromptu."

"Okay," said Rebecca, "but I'm going to introduce you anyway." With that, she tapped her glass with a spoon, getting everyone's attention.

"Hi everyone. Thank you so much for coming out this evening to meet Joseph. I hope you had an opportunity to hear his wonderful lecture earlier today. And I want to thank him for traveling here to join us this day."

With that, Rebecca stopped speaking and looked at Joseph. All eyes were on him. Joseph looked around the room but said nothing.

An awkward silence followed. The silence was broken when Joseph turned to the professors with whom he'd been engaged earlier and plunged back into conversation with them. He remained so engaged until nearly all guests had left.

Subsequently, Rebecca said to me: "Oh my goodness! When I think how close the search committee and I were to offering Joseph the position, I shudder. What a nightmare that would have been! Regarding the third profile characteristic, 'Interacts with members of the community to promote interest in and support for our program'—I don't think so!" Rebecca added, "As for the fourth, 'Collaborates with and supports the Director'—I *definitely* don't think so!"

Rebecca and her committee ultimately hired another finalist. Using the Star Profile as a discussion point, guide, and assessment tool, she found her star, who eventually succeeded her as program director.

One of the best things about using the Star Profile process is overcoming confirmation bias, which I describe in Chapter 2. Rebecca told me she and the committee were ready to offer Joseph the job without even considering the other finalists. His powerhouse credentials and powerhouse presentation were enough. Yet when Rebecca applied the Star Profile analysis, she saved herself and the Jewish Studies Department from making a big mistake.

STAR PROFILES HELP AVOID BIAS

The Star Profile process is also helpful with diversity, equity, and inclusion (DEI) initiatives. Implicit and confirmation biases tend to make us like what's most like us, whether it's race, creed, color, gender—or even passion for kids' soccer. By identifying ahead of time the core behaviors or actions that matter most and then scrupulously applying the process to evaluate the likelihood of fit, we avoid the bias trap that, among other flaws, works insidiously against DEI initiatives.

DISTINGUISHING GOOD AT CURRENT JOB FROM GOOD AT *NEW* JOB

Having previously made the mistake of assuming the salesperson with the best numbers necessarily should be promoted to sales manager, a Sales VP decided to use the Star Profile process. She created the following two profiles for a salesperson and a sales manager:

STAR SALESPERSON

1. Continuously stokes the pipeline to develop prospects and leads.

2. Becomes a great "closer" by understanding the customer's need—and the need behind the need.

3. Promptly and accurately reports all sales and expense data.

4. Collaborates well with customer service and accounting so that customer accounts get handled properly.

According to the Sales VP, the first sentence is essentially a reminder that no matter how well you may be doing at the time, a star salesperson doesn't neglect the pipeline. Otherwise, she says, "the well will eventually run dry."

The second sentence reflects a point of passion with the VP: "An existing or prospective customer may tell you what their need is, but there almost always is something unspoken—the need behind the need. If you can get to that level of understanding, you'll close the deal and build a relationship."

As for the third sentence, she says, "I don't care how good your sales numbers are if you don't promptly and accurately report them along with expenses you incur." She adds, "When salespeople don't do this, we end up having serious problems."

Regarding the last sentence, she says, "For us to work together, people in our sales department have to have good relationships with people in customer service and accounting. Unfortunately, we had a problem in the past with a big ego salesman who alienated people in these other departments. It became a real mess."

Here is the sales manager Star Profile:

STAR SALES MANAGER

1. Coaches sales staff to enable them to fulfill their Star Profiles.

2. Promotes a team-oriented spirit among sales staff, customer service, and accounting.

3. Keeps a vigilant eye on how we function, how our competitors function, and what's happening in the industry to sharpen our competitive edge.

"The key difference between the two profiles," the Sales VP says, "is that instead of focusing on just your own numbers, a star manager provides the kind of training, coaching, and other support that enables our salespeople to meet their star profiles."

As for the second sentence, she says, "I look to the manager to make sure that all three departments are functioning well together."

As for the last sentence, the VP explains that she needs a sales manager who maintains a big-picture focus. She gives an example: "Let's say we're a highly successful horse and buggy company, and the year is 1902. We better soon re-identify ourselves as a transportation company, or we're in for big trouble."

By creating these two profiles, the Sales VP can make a holistic assessment of each salesperson's performance and behavior in the context of the sales manager Star Profile. In essence, she avoids the Peter Principle (promote to the level of incompetence) and disables the Stupid Switch (by which the decision-makers make erroneous assumptions).

Avoiding an Internal Stupid Switch

The Star Profiles the Sales VP created are not just for use with external candidates. They allow her to have candid, constructive discussions with each internal candidate. Let's say she starts with her top salesperson. In my experience, a healthy, candid discussion of the difference between the two profiles will produce one of two outcomes: (1) the top salesperson declines the opportunity without bitterness or rancor or (2) she takes the job with a clear understanding of what's expected. To paraphrase the title of Marshall Goldsmith's best-selling book, she now knows that "what got you here won't [necessarily] get you there."

In his book *Hidden Potential: The Science of Achieving Greater Things,* Adam Grant states, "It's a mistake to judge people solely by the heights they've reached. By favoring applicants who have already excelled, selection systems underestimate and overlook candidates who are capable of greater things."[1] Grant shares a study of 38,000 salespeople where researchers found that the most successful sales numbers-wise were more likely to be promoted to manager. "But sales skills aren't the same as managerial skills," Grant explains. "Candidates who are better at closing deals are worse at managing people. Managers who elevated team performance weren't the biggest rainmakers. They were the most prosocial members as indicated by how often they made collaborative sales with their colleagues."[2]

INTEGRATING STAR PROFILES INTO HIRING AND PROMOTION PROCESSES

Here are the six steps I follow when using a Star Profile for hiring and promotion processes.

- **Step 1: Get proficient at crafting Star Profiles yourself.**
  Using the steps I describe in Chapter 5, craft and apply
  Star Profiles for every HR position in your organization,
  including yours. To talk the talk effectively, you've first got
  to walk it.

- **Step 2: Help your organization's leaders craft and apply Star Profiles for positions that report to them.** Work with them the way I work with organization leaders.

- **Step 3: Use the Star Profiles as recruitment and un-recruitment tools.** Paint the picture of behavioral success as early as possible. Recall from the Introduction my interview with Louonna. After we ended, she said, "Today's Friday. Can I start Monday?" By the same token, if you get a contrary response from a candidate, "If that's what you want, this job isn't for me," when's the best time to learn this? Of course, it's the *earliest*!

- **Step 4: Assess candidates' applications, materials submitted, and other information you have in light of the position's Star Profile.** Home in on this question: "Based on what I've reviewed, how confident am I that, once in the job, this person will meet behavioral expectations?"

- **Step 5: Train and coach your leaders.** Teach them how to use Star Profiles in interviews as follows:

  - Share each profile characteristic with the candidate, one characteristic at a time.

  - Invite a discussion of the characteristic using the EAR listening method from Chapter 2.

  - If the candidate says that the profile characteristic fits them, ask for specific past experiences that would indicate a potential fit.

- If the candidate's responses trigger your Spidey Sense that this may be another good-at-getting vs. good-at-doing candidate, ask for contact information for the people with knowledge of the experiences they share.
- Role plays work especially well in prepping your leaders for the interviews.

- **Step 6: Share and use the Star Profile in all hiring and promotion decisions.** When speaking with references and others with knowledge of the candidate, don't use formulaic questions like "Would you recommend this person?" Instead, share each profile characteristic and ask for the reference person's candid (and confidential) assessment of the likelihood that the candidate will meet the profile. I sometimes add, "Even though you may like and have high regard for Candidate X, if you truly don't think there's a likely fit, you're doing that person a favor by letting us know now." More than once, a reference person has responded with, "Please don't let X know, but if that's truly what you're seeking, it may not be a good fit."

STAR PROFILES HELP CULTURE COACHES IMPROVE HIRING AND PROMOTION

I've helped employers create and use Star Profiles for many different uses, even including compliance, claim prevention, and claim defense (discussed in Chapter 3). Yet, if I had to pick one use that provides more value than any other, it would be Star

Profiles used as employee selection and retention tools. After HR becomes adept at the process, it provides probably the best path for HR to be perceived by organization leaders as value-add versus cost-of-doing-business.

CHAPTER 8

No More Tomes!: Simplifying Policies and Onboarding

Years ago, I wrote an article for SHRM featuring five prominent California plaintiffs' attorneys. I asked them, "What's the principal cause of employment litigation?" None of them said "lack of compliance," i.e., failure to dot the compliance "i's" and cross the compliance "t's." All of them said it's because employees felt dehumanized, demoralized, and disrespected. That's what motivates them to seek a plaintiffs' attorney. The attorney then looks for compliance failures as ammunition for the claim that will be brought.

Do you know what makes people feel dehumanized? Being presented with a three-inch-thick binder (or the electronic equivalent) of company policies.

Since I first began practicing employment law in the early 1980s, HR policies have expanded exponentially. For the past couple of generations, it seems the operative HR move in response to any issue is "slap a policy on it!"

I once encountered a nineteen-page expense reimbursement policy. That's right—*nineteen pages!* Imagine your boss telling you, "I think it would be great for you to take a trip to the West Coast to visit our clients there." Dreading the thought of the reimbursement policy yet fearing you'll max out your credit cards, you reply, "Uh, boss, how about I just Zoom?"

Policy proliferation often substitutes for individual accountability. One or two employees misbehave in a certain way. Instead of dealing with them directly, HR creates a new policy to address the problem. As a result, *all* employees now have yet another rule to obey!

Policy proliferation undermines the manager–employee relationship. Instead of training, coaching, and empowering executives, managers, and supervisors to establish solid relationships with their reports, policy-plethora shifts the focus to rules, requirements, compliance, and consequences for violation. Instead of fostering human-to-human relationships, policy-plethora promotes shallow, transactional relationships: "I'll keep my head down and go through the motions to keep the paycheck coming—while keeping my eye out for something better."

Ironically, policy proliferation is another factor, like others I've previously discussed, that actually *increases* claim risk. Who's going to read a 34,000-word handbook? Not me! But there is one group that *will* read it: plaintiffs' lawyers. They're confident they can find inconsistencies between the handbook's words and reality, which can serve as the foundation to drive employee claims and litigation.

As I explain in the Introduction and Chapter 8, rabbit-like HR policy breeding is *not* due to risk *management*; it's due to risk *avoidance*. And it doesn't even accomplish that! That's why the Culture Coach approach is to focus on keeping things simple when it comes to policies and how (and when) they are communicated. That 34,000-word policy handbook? I helped that company reduce it to 2,200 words! In this chapter, I explain more about why minutiae-based policies are the antithesis of a Culture Coach and what to do instead.

LESS IS MORE & CUT THE LEGALESE: A CULTURE COACH APPROACH TO POLICIES

In recent years, many of my clients have complained about the difficulty in retaining employees and getting them to meet expectations, especially younger ones. They decry these employees' lack of commitment and stick-with-it-ness. Probably every generation has said that about the employees that follow. Currently, the primary "culprits" are Millennials and Gen Z. Soon, Gen Alpha will be added to the list.

Yet employers typically set the shallow, "business only" transactional tone at commencement of employment. One of the first things a new employee encounters is the requirement that they acknowledge that they have no contractual rights. The implied message is, "This handbook and the policies contained therein do not create any contractual obligations on the employer's part."

Next, the employee is required to acknowledge that their employment is at will. In other words, the company is saying, "Except for a reason prohibited by law, your employment may be terminated at any time for any or no reason, with or without notice, and with or without cause."

"Welcome!"

Contrast those traditional approaches with what Patty McCord, former chief operating officer of culture and chief product manager of people at Netflix, describes in her book *Powerful: Building a Culture of Freedom and Responsibility*. She began stripping away policies and procedures that took power away from employees. Examples included eliminating the vacation policy. Instead, employees were told to take the time they thought was appropriate and discuss it with their managers. She states in her book, "Trusting people to be responsible with their time was one of the early steps in giving them back their power."[1]

Another example is when McCord eliminated the company expense and travel policies. Instead, employees were told to use good judgment about how they spent the company's money. She states, "Again, we found the people didn't abuse the freedom. We saw that we could treat people like adults and that they loved it."[2]

In addition to less is more, let's cut the cold, harsh-sounding legalese. You can make your claim prevention point in more humanistic ways. Paul Buchanan, attorney with Buchanan Angeli Altschul & Sullivan in Portland, Oregon, represents employers and employees (although not at the same time). He shared with me a more humanistic "at will" disclaimer than traditional lawyer language:

> We hope and expect to have a long-term and mutually beneficial employment relationship. We recognize however that, at some point in the future, either you or the Company may choose to end the employment relationship. We believe that either party should be free to make that choice at any time. For this reason, employment at ABC company is at will, meaning either you or the company may choose to end the employment relationship at any time.[3]

Humanistic writing applies especially to health, disability, and leave-of-absence policies. They are intellectual puzzles that can be frustratingly complex for HR to administer and challenging to solve. Yet for the employee, it's emotional: "What happens if I or my family members get sick? What's the impact on my family and me?" Instead of allaying anxieties, your cold, dry, technical, compliance-focused policy provisions increase them. Both the wording *and* how HR administers these policies should instead be compassion-based.

Instead of beginning your handbook with legalistic disclaimers, how about beginning with a message like the following, which came from a company president:

> Dear Associates,
>
> I am humbled and honored to serve as president. This company was created with three purposes in mind: (1) create high-quality products that customers will greatly enjoy; (2) provide a safe, respectful, and healthy

work environment for our associates, enabling them to make a living, feel a sense of pride in their work, and support their families; and (3) generate profits that in part provide grants and other assistance to organizations serving women and children in impoverished and other at-risk circumstances.

I look forward to getting to know you. I am eager for you to apply your talents, energy, and initiative in supporting this wonderful company. Some leaders say they have an "open door" policy but don't really mean it. I do. If you ever have a question, issue, concern, or idea that you think will make us better, please contact me directly. This company isn't about me. It's about us!

Warmest regards,

[Name]

Instead of a ubiquitous dry contract disclaimer (*you have lots of responsibilities, but we don't*), how about saying something like the following:

Our Policies

This handbook contains many of our policies. They are not legal contracts between you and the company, but they do represent our philosophy, approach, and expectations. If at any time you have any questions about them, we encourage you to reach out to one of our human resources (HR) representatives.

Instead of jumping down the rabbit hole of rules, requirements, prohibitions, warnings, and disciplinary procedures, how about stating something like the following:

Core Behaviors

What do we expect from each of our associates in terms of performance, attendance, and conduct?

- Reliable and accountable: being where you need to be when you need to be there while doing what needs to get done for our success.

- Character and integrity: setting an example of honesty, hard work, dedication, and humility. This includes the willingness to accept constructive criticism, to give praise to others, and to continually be open to improvement.

- Support a coaching culture: meaning we're all on the same team trying to accomplish shared goals while cooperating and collaborating with each other to help our team win.

As you can see, I'm not recommending *no* HR policies. Rather, as Patty McCord did at Netflix, limit them to what is truly necessary or value-add. *And* express them in ways that show you truly care about your employees.

HUMANIZE ONBOARDING

It's your first day on the job.

After you walk into the building, anxiety overtakes excitement while you wait to be processed.

After you arrive, you're ushered into HR. You're walked through a bunch of rules, policies, and procedures. They include:

- The harshly worded, legalistic, zero-tolerance sexual harassment policy.

- The contractual disclaimer stating that although rules are mandatory for you, they're optional for the employer.

- Your acknowledgment of the "employment at-will" notice (except as prohibited by law, you can be fired at any time, with or without cause, reason, or notice).

After signing the forms and going through the compliance rigmarole, perhaps you'll have a similar experience as a friend had. After the compliance stuff, she was told, "If you want a desk, you'll have to assemble it yourself."

How's that for a first day! "Howdy, newcomer. Welcome aboard! Here's a screwdriver."

One of the changes made by Bruce Cutright, whose story as hospital CHRO I share in the Introduction, was how onboarding was handled. "New employees were told about HIPAA at least three times by three different presenters," he says. "I had one new employee tell me that he now knew that he couldn't breach patient confidentiality, but he didn't know where the bathroom was. We changed things up to require the new manager to meet and greet the employees on day one. This was a big improvement."

A Better Onboarding Story

My friend Micah Druckman shared with me this very different story about his onboarding experience. Prior to his start date at Oracle, his soon-to-be manager asked what type of laptop he wanted. Shortly thereafter, a member of Oracle's IT team called to confirm Micah's choice and promised to have it ready when he started.

Oracle's new-hire team invited Micah to an onboarding camp on his first day of work. It took place in a large conference room in Micah's building and consisted of a group of new employees and members of the new-hire team. After Micah received his new laptop ("I got the one I wanted!" he told me), the new-hire team efficiently led the group through the logistical details new employees need to know.

There was an icebreaker session and a talk about the organization's core values from a senior manager. Micah says the icebreaker session was a great way to learn about each other. The talk about core values was compelling; the manager gave several personal examples of how he has observed each value in action during his time at Oracle.

Next, new hires were greeted by their managers, walked to their desks, and introduced to new colleagues. Micah explained that they were given "two fantastic resources to help us with our onboarding after that first day: a chat channel to the new-hire team for any questions, which they replied to quickly and thoroughly, and a website with a new-hire checklist for our first day, week, and month at the job. The checklist includes links to important videos and policy documents to review, and each item can be checked off as it's completed."

One gesture that touched Micah personally: They were asked about special dietary needs, and Micah replied that he keeps kosher. In the middle of onboarding camp, a member of the new-hire team used a ride-hailing service to pick up his food and bring it back to him. "Her act made me feel valued on my first day at the company," Micah said.

CONDUCT A STAY INTERVIEW ON DAY ONE OR EARLIER

The "stay interview" has become popular in HR circles. It consists of asking current employees what keeps them coming to work and what might make them leave.

Why wait? How about asking employees on their first day or even earlier what attracted them to your company. And ask them what will make them happy they made the choice they did. Apply these three rules:

- The Golden Rule: Treat others as you would want to be treated.

- The Platinum Rule: Treat others the way they want to be treated.

- The Titanium Rule: Treat others the way they will most easily and naturally respond.

The "R" word should be "relationship," not "rules."

CULTURE COACHES ENCOURAGE THE POSITIVE

A Compliance Cop's role is to pay attention to everything negative that happens in an organization and make sure the company is protected from any legal consequences.

A Culture Coach, in contrast, sees their role as encouraging positive behaviors. So their approach to policy is to describe the best possible outcome (a long-term mutually beneficial relationship) rather than document the thousands of ways things can go wrong. They keep policies simple so they can be easily communicated and remembered. And they begin this work on Day One of employment so new hires feel welcomed into the organization.

CHAPTER 9

Minimize Harassment by Focusing on Civility, Not the Law

In 1986, the Supreme Court held that sexual harassment is a form of sex discrimination prohibited by Title VII of the Civil Rights Act of 1964. Harassment claims became big business when Congress, in 1991, amended the Civil Rights Act and created monetary damages in addition to back pay and allowed jury trials. Harassment claims began to proliferate.

Employers scrambled to respond. Sexual harassment prevention policies and training became a priority. As a management attorney, I was often asked to give presentations on the topic. Dressed in my darkest three-piece suit and power-red tie, I would lecture employees about the evils of workplace harassment and what would befall them if they were guilty: loss of job, career, reputation, and more. I shared the legalistic definitions provided by courts and the Equal Employment Opportunity Commission (EEOC). I told horror stories of actual cases, and I warned employees that retaliation and other forms of harassment were likewise prohibited and would not be tolerated.

No one seemed to enjoy these scare-you-straight presentations, including me. It's a drag speaking to a room full of sullen faces. One time in 1995, an employee stood up and started yelling, "This is communism! The government is taking away our rights!" He was led out of the room, and I continued with my spiel. Ugh!

Fast forward to today. Workplace sexual harassment is still very much a reality despite four decades of effort and an ocean of investment of time and money. Why? Aside from continuation of the mating instinct, the conventional approach to harassment prevention remains fundamentally misguided. In this chapter, I talk about why harassment prevention has been ineffective and provide a Culture Coach approach based on civility that can improve the working environment for all employees.

THE INEFFECTIVENESS OF HARASSMENT PREVENTION

During my career, I've dealt with innumerable sexual harassment situations. A key takeaway? In the overwhelming majority of cases, the harasser or alleged harasser didn't believe what he was doing constituted sexual harassment. (I use the male pronoun deliberately. Although I have dealt with a few cases in which the harasser was not male, the sexual harasser constituency continues to be dominated by the Y chromosome.)

Essentially, these men build up in their minds a set of rationalizations to tell themselves that what they're doing doesn't meet the legal harassment test. Therefore, they "reason," their behavior is perfectly acceptable. These rationalizations have been made even by serial predators who nonetheless persuaded themselves that they were innocent of any wrongdoing. They feel that what they're doing isn't "unwelcome." Rather, they're bringing light, joy, and happiness into the workplace or responding to their self-perceived sexiness. You'll often hear comments from these people such as, "I didn't mean anything by it!" or "It was just a little joke!" or "She encouraged it."

The reality of when and how harassment occurs in the workplace explains why most harassment prevention efforts are misguided:

1. It's based solely on deterrence: *If you engage in harassing behavior, there will be harsh consequences. Crime won't pay.* The people I met who rationalized their behavior didn't see it as harassment, so deterrence had no effect on them.

2. Behaviors are not deterred when people step onto the slippery slope. Harassers are like skiers on a slippery slope. They take an initial step out of line, most likely a small one. It might be an off-color comment or a compliment that goes a bit too far. No one says "No" or holds up an obvious stop sign. So they take another step, and another and another. Unbeknownst to them, the slope has changed.

They're now speeding downhill. Suddenly the cliff appears, and they can't stop in time. Crash!

3. Prevention efforts have also become increasingly complex because there are more categories of sex harassment now, including behavior based on sexual orientation and gender identity. People are bombarded by harassment messages and stop paying attention.

4. In addition, the conventional approach tends to be legalistic, focusing on the latest EEOC or court definitions of a hostile environment and quid pro quo harassment. Regular people—meaning any employee who hasn't studied the law in detail—have a hard time keeping track of all the technicalities.

There is another factor that compounds these issues: All of us have blind spots. Unfortunately, blind spots tend to grow as people move into positions of power. I recall a conversation with a CEO who bragged that at a company event, "Two good-looking young marketing assistants said, 'Jim, you're kind of sexy for an old guy.'"

"Jim," I replied, "they told you a half-truth." (I'll let you guess which half.)

On another occasion, a friend told me how, after he retired as CEO, he went back to work for the company in a part-time consulting capacity.

"I don't get it," he said. "They always used to laugh at my jokes. Now they don't."

"Bill," I replied, "that tells me one thing."

"What's that?" he asked.

"Your jokes weren't funny when you were CEO."

FRAME POLICIES AROUND CIVILITY

If you google "Sexual Harassment Policy," you'll find dozens of suggested documents that, in my view, are counterproductive, to put it kindly. Overwhelmingly, they track the conventional legalistic deterrence approach.

The late US Supreme Court Justice Antonin Scalia stated in a 1998 decision that anti-discrimination laws were not intended to expand "into a general civility code for the American workplace."[1] Yet civility is exactly what's needed.

Paul Buchanan, an employment law attorney in Portland, Oregon, whose more-humane "at will" statement I shared previously, notes that when employers maintain a standard of mutual respect and an expectation that employees treat others with dignity, they are very unlikely to find themselves crossing legal lines into unlawful discriminatory harassment of any kind.

He adds to this sentiment by saying that adopting a standard of civility makes sense from all kinds of perspectives—only one of which is a legal perspective, and that's not even the most important one, in my view—to train and expect employees at all levels of the organization to meet a much higher threshold of conduct than not violating laws on harassment and discrimination.

I fully endorse creating a "standard of civility" because the goal of a Culture Coach is not just to reduce or prevent harassment, but to create a workplace environment where every employee can contribute their fullest. That's what will help the business achieve peak performance. And it won't happen if people feel unsafe in any sense of that word. What does a civility policy look like? Here's my recommendation.

ESTABLISH A STANDARD OF CIVILITY: COMMITMENT TO MUTUAL RESPECT, PROFESSIONALISM, & CIVILITY

When it comes to treatment of others, we set the bar high. We believe that all employees are entitled to a safe and secure work environment where we treat each other with respect, professionalism, and civility always. This policy expresses the commitment we've made to create and maintain such an environment.

COMMENTARY: Set the bar high here—not at legal compliance. Striving for respectful treatment will prevent a lot of disruptive behavior, not just harassment. This approach still encompasses compliance yet is much more ambitious and healthier overall for the organization.

WHAT WE EXPECT OF EACH OTHER

We treat all employees, vendors, clients, customers, and guests—and anyone else with whom we interact—with respect, professionalism, and civility always. This means exercising emotional self-control and sensitivity to the feelings of others. When differences arise, address them with a constructive, problem-solving approach, not with blame or judgment.

Avoid slippery slopes where we may think our behavior is acceptable even though it falls short of professionalism, civility, and respect. Avoid rationalizations or excuses such as "It was consensual," "I wasn't the first to tell an off-color joke," "I only made fun of my own race," "No one complained or seemed uncomfortable," or "My behavior was no different than theirs."

Also, retaliation is never acceptable, which we define as taking *any* form of negative action against someone who raises a concern.

COMMENTARY: Disregard the Supreme Court's definition of legally actionable retaliation. Any form of hostility should be promptly confronted.

continued

Conduct that falls short of civility, professionalism, and respect should always be addressed. If we are subject to or witness disrespectful or offensive conduct, here are some options:

COMMENTARY: This policy encourages bystanders to report problematic behavior—not as tattling, but as each person's commitment to ensuring a psychologically and physically safe workplace for everyone.

Option A

In some circumstances, directly confronting the offender can be effective. If you are comfortable doing so, you matter-of-factly: (1) Point out the specific behavior; (2) Briefly describe its impact, e.g., "When you say _____, it makes me uncomfortable"; and (3) Ask the person not to repeat this behavior.

Note: Option A is never required. You can always select a different option.

COMMENTARY: In my experience, a substantial majority of sexual harassment problems could have been avoided if the person who was offended gave an early unequivocal message, such as, "This behavior makes me uncomfortable. Please stop."

Yet, in pretty much every major harassment problem I've dealt with, such self-help was not attempted. Whether it's a natural reluctance to confront others, a fear of retaliation, or a tendency toward rationalization ("Maybe he'll get the hint and stop on his own"), opportunities are lost to stop minor problems before they become major.

The key is to ensure that the policy also says self-help is not required and makes it clear that if self-help doesn't work, reporting options should be invoked. Acquiescence is never appropriate.

Option B

Talk to a member of our HR team or anyone in a leadership position. It doesn't have to be your supervisor. They will work with you to find the best solution to the problem.

COMMENTARY: Support of this policy should not be HR's exclusive domain. Anyone and everyone in a supervisory position should be taught and coached on what to do when they become aware of a problem. This approach maximizes the likelihood that an employee will come forward versus bottling up the problem. It also helps leadership avoid the growth-in-authority/growth-in-blind-spot spiral.

My alternative policy and approach may make your employment law attorney nervous. However, I was told by a then-EEOC Commissioner and a then-EEOC General Counsel that they really liked my policy even though they couldn't comment publicly.

Nevertheless, if your attorney thinks it's necessary, stick the conventional language in your handbook somewhere. However, when it comes to application, use your civility policy.

FROM DOCUMENT TO PRACTICE: MAKING CIVILITY COME ALIVE

A civility policy, even a perfectly worded one, is not a magic pill. By itself alone, it won't change the culture. Perhaps Gretchen Carlson, a former Fox News journalist who filed a harassment case against Roger Ailes, then-chairman and CEO of the network, put it best: "When it comes to workplace behavior, the buck stops at the top."[2]

It's essential that organization leaders model the desired behavior. Don't just tell HR to hold a class on the topic. This ancient piece of wisdom especially applies here: Practice what you preach.

INTERNAL INVESTIGATIONS SHOULD FOCUS ON SOLVING PROBLEMS

Too often, when an internal harassment problem arises, HR takes an overly technical and legalistic approach, which tends to ratchet up tension and fear. In its quest to avoid legal risk, HR often unwittingly raises anxiety and even claim risk.

Internal investigations should never be about staying out of court. They should be about solving problems with the overall objective of *preserving* or *restoring* workplace physical and psychological safety.

When making your findings, don't ever say "sexual harassment." That term is a legal conclusion. At the internal investigation stage, it's neither necessary nor even productive to use it.

In my law practice days, I had an embarrassing exchange with a judge.

I filed a motion for summary judgment, arguing that the conduct in question did not meet the sexual harassment test as a matter of law.

"Excuse me, Mr. Janove," the judge said. "You're telling me that this conduct, while offensive, is not sexual harassment as the law defines it. Is that correct?"

"Yes, Your Honor."

"Are you aware that your client's HR department reached the opposite conclusion?"

"Uh, yes, Your Honor, but I'd like to further state that . . ."

"Motion denied!"

(I'd like to say that was my only embarrassing exchange as a lawyer with a judge, but perhaps that's why I'm now a coach and consultant instead.)

Going back to Covey's "begin with the end in mind" advice, that end goal is simple and straightforward: Find out what more likely than not occurred (the behavior), how this behavior impacted others, and assess what the best solution would be to restore a healthy work environment going forward.

Even if you're positive that the legal harassment test is met, don't say so. By the same token, don't use conclusory words like "bullying." Simply point out the behavior and its impact, cite the relevant organization policies or values, and make your recommendation as to what the appropriate solution should be. Leave the law to the lawyers. Along these lines, I recommend replacing the words "investigations," "findings," and "conclusions" with "assessment" and "recommendations."

With this in mind, an appropriate conclusory statement might be something like this: We have completed our review and have the following assessment: Employee X violated the company's _____ Policy. As such, we are taking action consistent with that policy.

CIVILITY PREVENTS MANY PROBLEMS

Workplace sexual and other harassment can be eradicated. However, that won't happen until and unless organizations change the current paradigm of focusing on compliance, claim prevention, and claim defense. If you continue with that paradigm, you'll get the same results that companies have gotten for the past four decades—no significant lasting progress and continuing harassment claims.

Instead, take the Culture Coach approach to creating a workplace environment that focuses on civility, respect, and professionalism. Doing so will reduce (with the goal of eliminating) not only harassment behaviors but also other kinds of demeaning or dismissive behavior. And remember that the tone and tenor of any workplace culture starts at the top, so ensure your leaders are modeling only the most professional, respectful behavior.

CHAPTER 10

Inclusion: Replace Preaching with Practice

Years ago, when I was an office managing shareholder in a large international firm, we would have periodic get-togethers with fellow office managing shareholders to review various developments. Usually, our sessions included a presentation or workshop on DEI (Diversity, Equity, and Inclusion).

During these programs, I remember looking around the room and seeing mostly white male faces while a woman or person of color presented on the topic. Unfortunately, I never got a sense from these presentations that any important message had landed. We'd listen politely, if not enthusiastically, and then return to our normal business.

DEI efforts have been under scrutiny in recent years, with

some companies formally scaling back efforts they labeled as DEI. In fact, not without some controversy, SHRM has replaced DEI with I&D, dropping "Equity" and now leading with "Inclusion." Its president and CEO, Johnny C. Taylor Jr., SHRM-SCP, explains that diversity is inevitable given demographics; the key now is inclusion. I agree. This chapter describes my suggestions for making true inclusion a reality.

DIVERSITY WITHOUT INCLUSION

A friend of mine was general counsel (GC) of a large company. He invited several national law firms to make presentations for why they should get his company's legal business. One thing the GC stressed was DEI.

Each firm submitted a detailed proposal and dispatched a team of attorneys to visit the company's headquarters. Each firm laid it on thick about how strongly they value inclusion and diversity. At each in-person presentation, there was always at least one woman and someone of color. Each PowerPoint deck strongly featured diverse faces and diversity commitments.

Despite the DEI emphasis, after the company selected a firm, the GC discovered reality was different. "Thereafter," he said, "it seemed like every time we had a need for legal services, a white male attorney got the assignment."

I checked the attorney directory for this large firm's website. There were plenty of women and minority attorneys listed. Yet, until the GC complained, none of them got the work.

That's what I call diversity *without* inclusion.

Inclusion Includes White Men

The lack of women and minorities in the preceding example has a flipside that is not always publicly acknowledged. A big problem with DEI initiatives is that they reveal their own implicit bias. DEI professionals may not be saying this, but they're probably thinking it: "The obstacle is white men with disproportionate power and influence. The goal is to overcome this obstacle."

Speaking as a white male, if that's the vibe I get from you, I'll feel anything but "included." Don't expect my support. Resentment and resistance are more likely.

I once participated in a Zoom forum on workplace conflict. The topic shifted to conflict based on racial differences. I began to offer my perspective as an attorney who dealt with many race discrimination and race harassment cases. An African American woman cut me off. Puzzled, I asked why. "You don't know, and you can't understand," she said. No one spoke up in my defense. I shut up and tuned out.

No one wants to feel marginalized or canceled, white men included. I don't like being the only one expected to acknowledge my biases when everyone has them. I don't like being the only person it's okay to stereotype. And I don't like the suggestion that my career success is due primarily to my race and gender.

A NEW INCLUSION STRATEGY

An inclusion strategy should start with a holistic message about the benefits to everyone of a more diverse workforce. There is ample evidence that diversity improves organizational health, benefiting everyone, including white men. Make it clear that the DEI initiative is not a zero-sum game with white guys being the zero.

That said, my next advice is to create a specific white male inclusion strategy that engages that demographic in implementing the policies. Seek out white men to participate in your initiative. For example, when one of my clients formed a DEI committee, a high-ranking white man was recruited to be co-chair. This move later proved crucial when challenging messages needed to be communicated to the predominantly white male leadership group.

Kay Toran, CEO of the Oregon chapter of Volunteers of America, is passionate about creating diversity-rich, inclusive workplace cultures. When I interviewed her in 2024, she noted that DEI initiatives often mistakenly fail to reach out to white male employees. She recommends actively engaging white males in the process. "Frankly, as an African American woman, I'm probably less effective than a white male in reaching out to another white male. We need to be open to what interventions work most effectively at building trust and respect across race, color, origin, gender, and other lines."[1]

FIVE INCLUSION LESSONS FROM BASKETBALL

Many highly successful sports teams are also highly diverse, including by race, religion, national origin, economic and cultural background, primary language, and sexual orientation. Yet these differences are in no way impediments to team success and the feeling of team oneness. What is it about team sports that makes achieving DEI so much easier and more effective? What lessons can employers learn? Here are a few characteristics that differentiate the typical workplace from a sports team.

1. Clear Goals Shared

In team sports, the goal is clear: win. Everyone, from coaches and players to administrators and support staff, cares about and shares the same goal of winning. They also share steppingstone goals—the various steps and signposts necessary to achieve the goal.

Team leaders make it their mission to ensure a collective understanding of and commitment to the same goals. By contrast, employees in most companies either lack a clear understanding of the organization's goals, or the goals are uninspiring. As a worker, how am I supposed to get fired up about shareholder ROI?

2. Measuring What Matters (Even the "Small" Stuff)

Sports teams don't waste time measuring meaningless subjective performance metrics. Don't expect the Los Angeles Lakers to give LeBron James an annual performance review. "Uh, LeBron, for this season, we rate you a 3.0. Please try harder next season."

Sports teams continually identify and measure the metrics that matter, not just "box score" stuff, but the things that can be just as important, e.g., screens set, charges taken, proper rotations made, shots contested, and the so-called hockey assist (the pass that leads to the pass that leads to the basket).

3. Maximizing Strengths

How often have you had a boss ask, "How can I maximize your talents to help you succeed?" More likely, you were given a detailed job description to review and to which you were expected to conform. Your boss didn't adapt to you. You did the adapting. That approach leads to "that's not my job" thinking, as well as "that's how we've always done it here." Rigidity prevails.

My late friend Mark Eaton finished his college basketball career at UCLA sitting on the bench. UCLA's new coach didn't believe he could fit in. Eaton figured he got a free college education and prepared to return to his former job as an auto mechanic.

However, his community college coach knew the Utah Jazz coach Frank Layden and called him and said Mark was worth investing in. The Jazz took a chance on what they called "a project." Mark worked diligently on his biggest strength, which was, as the legendary Wilt Chamberlain had advised Mark, "to protect the paint."

Eaton's jersey (No. 53) hangs in the rafters at the Utah Jazz's stadium along with other all-time Jazz greats. He still holds the NBA record for blocked shots in a season.

4. Accountability at All Levels

In most companies, accountability tends to be transactional: "Follow the rules and keep your job." On good sports teams, accountability takes a different tack and starts at the individual level. Each player feels a personal obligation to support the team.

Notice how often, when asked, the star of the losing team says, "I have to get better." It's not "them"—it's "I."

Accountability also extends from team member to team member. There is a willingness to call out a colleague if needed for the betterment of the team. And the coach represents ultimate accountability. From individual to peer to authority figure, accountability pervades.

5. Discipline and Discharge

In team sports, there's no margin for letting things fester. If you're underperforming, your coach will proactively let you know what the gap is between what's needed and where you are—no ambiguity and no avoidance. Also, there's no "first, second, third warning" nonsense. "Caitlin Clark, you shot two for twelve in yesterday's game. Therefore, we are putting you on a PIP (Performance Improvement Plan)."

If a player is cut, it's not because the player is a failed human being. It's because the coach believes there's someone else who can better help the team win.

To create DEI-rich work environments, organization leaders need to start thinking like coaches.

THE CASE FOR STRATEGIC INCREMENTAL IMPLEMENTATION STEPS

The Culture Coach mentality forces us to consider the big picture of how our goals can be achieved. In this case, to be effective, DEI needs to be part of a disciplined strategic planning process. Key metrics need to be identified, such as the demographics of who holds what positions and at what compensation levels. More than just the obvious numbers, however, the due diligence component of strategic DEI planning should include a close assessment of how employee selection decisions are made and how careers are advanced.

For example, consider my former career. I founded my own law firm and became what's known in the trade as a rainmaker, meaning I generated enough work to keep myself and other attorneys, paralegals, and support staff busy. How did I get there? Talent? Perhaps a smidge. Luck? Certainly. Critical mentorship? Absolutely!

When I was a young attorney in a large law firm, two senior partners took an interest in me. They gave me opportunities for face time with clients and increasingly responsible roles at trials and other legal proceedings. I got included on business trips and client pitches, and advice, instruction, and correction for my many mistakes. These two partners were essential to my rise as an attorney and eventually to my being able to launch my own firm. As you might suspect, both attorneys were older white men.

When a DEI initiative is being pursued in an organization where white men still disproportionately hold positions of power, accountability has to work in all directions. And at one end, resistance must be confronted. If you have a senior white man in a key position who is actively or passively resisting the DEI initiative, he needs to know that it is a nonnegotiable organizational commitment. If it's not for him, he needs to go someplace else.

EXPECTATIONS
REMAIN THE SAME

As people besides white men are put into decision-making positions, it needs to be clear that performance expectations remain the same. HR and other leaders should be vigilant to ensure there isn't an avoidance problem in which a white male manager avoids confronting a subordinate employee due to fear of being accused of racism, sexism, or other ism.

A DEI Implementation Example

I worked with a white male–dominated professional services firm that decided, especially for business reasons, to adopt a DEI initiative. A DEI committee was formed, co-chaired by a female partner and a male partner.

The committee created a list of all other committees and their members. It proposed timetables by which women and people of color would be added and, subsequently, would be made committee chairs.

Successes were publicized internally. These included 1) a white male committee chair saying "I was looking for a successor" and passing the chair to a female committee member; 2) a white male partner who let the firm's leaders know he brought a young associate of color on an important client visit and that he did very well; and 3) a passionate "anti-woke" white male conservative who shared that he found it beneficial to tout the firm's DEI initiative to existing and prospective clients.

The firm's initiative and approach produced lasting positive results. There weren't any grand, inspiring speeches, and it wasn't an overnight success. Yet, with diligence, perseverance, and attention to detail, the tide raised all ships.

INCLUSION FOR EFFECTIVENESS

If there was ever a case to be made for the saying "It's better to be effective than to be right," it's the DEI field. Unfortunately, too many well-meaning people lean toward being right versus being effective. Yet, if you truly want both a diverse and an inclusive workforce, it's incumbent on you to replace preaching with practice and to focus on the small steps that, over time, will lead to big results.

Conclusion

H R can be a fantastic profession with unlimited upside. What's needed is a paradigm shift. A shift that takes imagination and initiative. Instead of HR making compliance first, let's make it *third*—after cultural health and people development. Instead of a cost of doing business, HR can and should be an investment paying major dividends in an organization's health and success.

Thus far, this book has pointed out the benefits to organizations when HR shifts from a compliance/claim prevention paradigm to a people culture paradigm. Yet the benefits of this change go well beyond the workplace. As noted in the book *We: How to Increase Performance and Profits Through Full Engagement* by Rudy Karsan and Kevin Kruse, an Iowa State University research team studied 337 families in northern Iowa over a four-year period. Researchers reported what they called "the Spillover Effect." They found that "a spouse's job exerts as much influence on individual distress levels as does conflict from one's own job."[1] They found that when an employee shares their work frustration with their spouse, their stress level doesn't go down. Instead, the spouse's stress level rises to meet theirs. How's that for a Win-Win proposition? "Gee honey, thanks for sharing!"

As I mention in the Introduction, I began this book as one of criticism, detailing the wrong turn the HR profession took beginning about forty years ago. Yet, thanks to the work of many amazing HR and organization leaders, this book has evolved into one of hope. The changes I recommend won't just cure HR burnout (see the sidebar). They'll make workplaces healthier and more successful, *and* they will do good in the world.

AVOIDING HR BURNOUT

Perhaps the most effective way to avoid HR burnout is to get to know your organization's business. Follow Alan Mulally, whom I mention in Chapter 1, and develop a sense of curiosity about all the different things that go into your organization's mission and functioning. As I described in a SHRM article, many HR professionals have benefited greatly from job rotation programs where they temporarily serve as nurse aids, customer service representatives, auto parts salespeople, line manufacturing workers, accounting clerks, and many other jobs. What they learn pays off in their own job effectiveness while cementing trust and understanding.

In my job as organization development consultant and executive leadership coach, I've repeatedly experienced the happy results of change *outside the workplace*. In addition to no longer bringing home negative stress, organization leaders and employees apply practices such as the No-FEAR conversation, the EAR, the MIDAS Touch, and others in family, community, and other non-work situations. Again, and again, I hear about the positive impact. Even the Star Profile has played a role outside the workplace. Among other things, it's been used to help couples decide whether to marry and, if so, to stay married.

My hope for this book, dear reader, is transformation. One in which people do good for themselves and for others. Perhaps George Eliot's (Mary Ann Evans) end to her magnificent novel *Middlemarch* fits here: "The growing good of the world is partly dependent on unhistoric acts; and that things are not so ill with you and me as they might have been, is half owing to the number who lived faithfully a hidden life, and rest in unvisited tombs."[2]

Acknowledgments

If I were to name everyone who contributed to this book, directly or indirectly, the list would be enormous—and I'd be paranoid about the people I'd undoubtedly fail to include. Suffice it to say: It took a village to write this book, and I am most grateful to each and every village member.

I'll add that it's been a great experience working with the Greenleaf team. If you're an author looking for a publisher that takes a collaborative approach to book publishing, you can't go wrong with Greenleaf.

Notes

INTRODUCTION

1. Edgar Allan Poe, "The Cask of Amontillado," in *Godey's Lady's Book*, November 1846.

2. Judith Droz Keyes, "The Case for Eliminating Performance Reviews," SHRM, March 30, 2011.

3. Jon Clifton and Patrick Bogart, "40 Top Workplaces You'll Want to Get to Know," Gallup, March 28, 2019, https://www.gallup.com/workplace/248066/top-workplaces-know.aspx/.

4. Bruce Cutright in conversation with the author, November 2024.

CHAPTER 1

1. Jathan Janove, "An American Icon Talks HR," SHRM, September 1, 2020, https://www.shrm.org/topics-tools/news/humanity-hr-compliance/american-icon-talks-hr/.

2. Janove, "An American Icon Talks HR."

3. Janove, "An American Icon Talks HR."

4. Janove, "An American Icon Talks HR."

5. Janove, "An American Icon Talks HR."

6. Johnny C. Taylor Jr., email message to author, October 2024.

7. Christine Porath and Douglas R. Conant, "The Key to Campbell Soup's Turnaround? Civility," *Harvard Business Review*, October 5, 2017, https://hbr.org/2017/10/the-key -to-campbell-soups-turnaround-civility/.

8. Jathan Janove, "Doug Conant: How CEOs and HR Can Work Together Successfully," SHRM, February 18, 2022, https ://www.shrm.org/topics-tools/news/employee-relations /doug-conant-how-ceos-hr-can-work-together-successfully/.

9. Janove, "Doug Conant."

10. Jathan Janove, "Courage, Humility, & Organization Leadership," Marshall Goldsmith, December 18, 2020, https://scc.mgscc.net/index.php/2020/12/18/courage -humility-organization-leadership/.

11. Art Kleiner, "The Thought Leader Interview: Douglas Conant," *strategy+business*, August 28, 2012, https://www .strategy-business.com/article/00128/.

CHAPTER 2

1. Jathan Janove, "The Cure for HR Burnout," SHRM, September 19, 2023, https://www.shrm.org/topics-tools /news/humanity-hr-compliance/cure-hr-burnout/.

2. Greg Lewis, "The Jobs with the Highest Turnover Rates, According to LinkedIn Data," LinkedIn Talent Blog, June 30,

2022, https://www.linkedin.com/business/talent/blog/talent
-analytics/types-of-jobs-with-most-turnover/.

3. Response to "What are the essential traits of an executive
   coach?" https://marshallgoldsmith.ai/chat, November 2024.

4. David French, "To Support Ukraine, Persuade the Elephant,"
   New York Times, December 14, 2023, https://www.nytimes.com
   /2023/12/14/opinion/america-ukraine-russia-support.html/.

5. Response to "How can coaching help the HR profession?"
   https://marshallgoldsmith.ai/chat, December 15, 2024.

CHAPTER 3

1. "Habit 2: Begin With the End in Mind," Franklin Covey
   Benelux, https://www.franklincovey-benelux.com/en
   /resources/habit-2-begin-with-the-end-in-mind/.

2. John Parauda and Jathan Janove, "Legal Trends: Early
   Settlement," SHRM, November 1, 2004, https://www
   .shrm.org/topics-tools/news/hr-magazine/legal-trends-early
   -settlement/.

3. Abraham Lincoln, "Notes for a Law Lecture," document
   fragment dated July 1, 1850, https://www.abrahamlincolnon
   line.org/lincoln/speeches/lawlect.htm/.

CHAPTER 4

1. Lecture attended by the author, SHRM Annual Conference
   2015.

CHAPTER 5

1. Ben Wigert and Heather Barrett, "2% of CHROs Think Their Performance Management System Works," Gallup, May 7, 2024, https://www.gallup.com/workplace/644717/chros -think-performance-management-system-works.aspx/.

2. Patty McCord, *Powerful: Building a Culture of Freedom and Responsibility* (Silicon Guild, 2018) 113.

3. Daniel Pink, email message to author, October 2024.

CHAPTER 6

1. Jathan Janove, "Demote Demotions," SHRM, May 12, 2022, https://www.shrm.org/topics-tools/news/humanity-hr -compliance/demote-demotions/.

CHAPTER 7

1. Adam Grant, *Hidden Potential: The Science of Achieving Greater Things* (Viking, 2023) 292.

2. Grant, *Hidden Potential*, 296.

CHAPTER 8

1. Patty McCord, *Powerful: Building a Culture of Freedom and Responsibility* (Silicon Guild, 2018) 8.

2. McCord, *Powerful*, 9.

3. Remember that nothing in this book contains legal advice. In Chapter 3, I share with you tips on how to engage an employment law attorney where the goal is risk management, *not* avoidance.

CHAPTER 9

1. Oncale v. Sundowner Offshore Services, Inc., 523 U.S. 75 (1998).

2. Jathan Janove, "Jerks at Work No More!" SHRM, September 1, 2021, https://www.shrm.org/topics-tools/news/humanity -hr-compliance/jerks-work-no-more/.

CHAPTER 10

1. Kay Toran in conversation with the author, April 2024.

CONCLUSION

1. Rudy Karsan and Kevin Kruse, *We: How to Increase Performance and Profits Through Full Engagement* (Tantor Media, 2011) 42.

2. George Eliot, *Middlemarch* (Little Brown & Co., 1900) 841.

About the Author

For the first twenty-five years of his career, Jathan Janove, a graduate of the University of Chicago Law School, practiced employment law, initially representing employees and unions and later switching to the management side. He was licensed in six states. In 2005, the Utah State Bar named him "Employment Lawyer of the Year," and in 2006, the J. Reuben Clark Law Society—Salt Lake Chapter named him "Citizen Lawyer of the Year."

Since leaving the practice of law, Jathan has served as an organization development consultant and executive coach with a focus on workplace culture and human capital development. He is a Master Coach for the international Marshall Goldsmith Stakeholder Centered Coaching organization and writes its "Ask the Coach" column (https://knowledgebank.mgscc.net/ask-the-coach/). He is a longtime speaker and writer for SHRM and writes the column "Putting Humanity into HR Compliance." He served three years as president of the Organization Development Network—Oregon.

He lives in Portland, Oregon, and can be contacted through his website: www.jathanjanove.com.

Other Books
by the Author

Hard-Won Wisdom: True Stories from the Management Trenches

Breakthrough: How Stakeholder Centered Coaching Transformed the Executive Coaching Industry

Coaching Stories to Inspire Change (Chief Editor)

Remembering Bert Spiegel

The Star Profile: A Management Tool to Unleash Employee Potential

Managing to Stay Out of Court: How to Avoid the Eight Deadly Sins of Mismanagement

www.ingramcontent.com/pod-product-compliance
Lightning Source LLC
Chambersburg PA
CBHW031851200326
41597CB00012B/370